Unclogging the Arteries

The Impact of Transport Costs on Latin American and Caribbean Trade

Mauricio Mesquita Moreira
Christian Volpe
Juan S. Blyde

Special Report on Integration and Trade

Inter-American Development Bank

David Rockefeller Center for Latin American Studies
Harvard University

1300 New York Avenue, N.W.
Washington, D.C. 20577

Co-published by
David Rockefeller Center for Latin American Studies
Harvard University
1730 Cambridge Street
Cambridge, MA 02138

Produced by the IDB Office of External Relations

Distributed by Harvard University Press
www.hup.harvard.edu

Cataloging-in-Publication data provided by the
Inter-American Development Bank
Felipe Herrera Library

Moreira, Mauricio Mesquita.
Unclogging the arteries : the impact of transport costs on Latin American and Caribbean trade / Mauricio Mesquita Moreira, Christian Volpe, Juan S. Blyde.

p. cm.
Includes bibliographical references.
ISBN: 978-1-59782-074-5

1. Transportation—Latin America—Costs. 2. Transportation—Caribbean Area—Costs. 3. Freight and freightage—Costs. 4. Transportation and state. I. Volpe, Christian. II. Blyde, Juan S. III. Inter-American Development Bank. IV. David Rockefeller Center for Latin American Studies.

HE215.5 .M582 2008
380.5098 M582—dc22 LCCN: 2008929436

Table of Contents

Prologue

International trade is widely recognized as one of the most important drivers of economic development. More integrated markets facilitate the free flow of goods and factors across borders allowing countries to benefit from a better reallocation of resources. Access to more customers permits exporters to exploit economies of scale, and more open markets foster competition, encourage innovation and productivity and expand choice for consumers and inputs for producers. Today, countries in Latin America and the Caribbean recognize the increasingly important role that integration plays in their development.

During the last decades, the countries in the region have come a long way in opening their markets by reducing traditional barriers to trade, such as tariffs. Despite this progress, the integration agenda remains daunting. Some of the traditional barriers to trade still remain high in certain sectors, markets and countries of the region, while there are many other obstacles that limit the integration of markets, not only for goods but also for factors. Many of these obstacles take the form, for example, of bottlenecks behind borders that act as informal trade barriers. Identifying the remaining barriers and quantifying their impacts are, in many ways, much more difficult tasks than assessing the impact of traditional border measures, like tariffs. The implication of this is clear; there is a challenge to produce more and better technical analyses to locate where the bottlenecks are that still preclude countries from deepening their integration efforts.

A priority for the Inter-American Development Bank is to help countries in Latin America and the Caribbean face this challenge, not only from an analytical perspective but also in terms of policies and operations. The Bank is committed to support the region with high-quality products that help them identify the obstacles to integration and design policies to address them.

Unclogging the Arteries: The Impact of Transport Costs on Latin American and Caribbean Trade exemplifies this commitment and is the first in a series of reports that the Integration and Trade Sector of the Inter-American

Development Bank is preparing on this important agenda. The report combines a robust technical analysis using large and detailed databases with a series of case studies that provide vivid accounts of the problems on the ground. This combination of approaches gives a comprehensive view of the significance of transport costs as a barrier to trade in the region. The report calls for a broader and more balanced integration agenda, which would focus not only on the traditional barriers to trade, but also on costs, such as those associated with transport-related infrastructure.

Santiago Levy Algazi
Vice President for Sectors and Knowledge, IDB

Antoni Estevadeordal
Manager of Integration and Trade Sector, IDB

Acknowledgments

Unclogging the Arteries: The Impact of Transport Costs on Latin American and Caribbean Trade is the product of a collaborative research effort within the Integration and Trade Sector of the Inter-American Development Bank.

The author for Chapter 1 was Mauricio Mesquita Moreira, for Chapter 2, Juan S. Blyde, and for Chapter 3, Christian Volpe. Mauricio Mesquita Moreira and Juan S. Blyde wrote Chapter 4, based on the case studies prepared by Henry Vega (Ecuador), Jorge Chami Batista (Brazil), Ricardo Sicra (Argentina), and Enrique Dussel Peters (Mexico).

This effort would not have been possible without the intellectual and material support of Antoni Estevadeordal, Manager of the Integration and Trade Sector, and the technical supervision of David Hummels, Professor of Economics at the Krannert School of Management, Purdue University. Mr. Hummels' extensive and groundbreaking work on transport costs, as well as his insightful comments, greatly benefited this report.

Rafael Cornejo played an instrumental role in putting together the database that supports the findings herein, and Marco Antonio Martínez del Angel and Jerónimo Carballo provided excellent research assistance. Ricardo Carciofi and José Pineda also contributed with constructive comments to an earlier version of this report.

The research team would like to thank the Latin American Association of Foreign Trade (ALADI) for granting them access to a very detailed and comprehensive database on freight rates and import tariffs in Latin America and the Caribbean. Special thanks also goes to Thomas Cornelissen, for kindly providing the STATA program to implement the four-way error component model, and Rodrigo Salas, for making it possible for the team to process vast amounts of data.

Introduction

The trade policy agenda of Latin America and the Caribbean (LAC) in the last two decades has been mainly focused on traditional market access and policy barrier issues. Whereas this emphasis was justifiable in the earlier nineties—tariffs and non-tariff barriers were clearly the main obstacle to trade—the region now faces a different reality. For one thing, multilateral negotiations, unilateral trade liberalizations and preferential agreements have brought policy-related trade costs to a fraction of what they were in the past and even though they are still unduly high in some sectors, markets and countries, the immediate consequence is that the relevance of other, less visible trade costs has increased over time.

For another, LAC now faces a new world economy, which bears little resemblance to the one that prevailed in the eighties and early nineties. The combination of trade liberalization, which has brought vast countries such as China and India into the world markets, fast technological development, and falling communication and transport costs has reshaped countries' comparative advantages and has imposed a much higher penalty for economies that are complacent about high trade costs.

This new reality calls for a more balanced trade agenda, with governments, international institutions and researchers putting more resources into measuring, identifying causes, understanding the impact and developing policies to minimize non-policy trade costs. The pressing need for this new agenda is clear for both intra- and extraregional trade. Without, for instance, improving a poor transport infrastructure, whose development was biased towards extraregional markets by centuries of colonial rule based on resource exploitation, and that has suffered badly from underinvestment in the last decades, it is unlikely that LAC will maximize the gains of scale and specialization that can arise from the growing number of preferential agreements being signed at home.

Likewise, to expand and diversify its exports and take full advantage of the increasing fragmentation of production and time-sensitiveness of international trade, LAC can no longer rely solely on trade agreements, proximity, labor costs and on an abundant supply of natural resources. Having much higher labor costs than Asia (and lower productivity growth) (IDB 2006) and having its geographic advantage being eroded by rapidly falling air freight rates (Hummels 2007) and by economies of scale and oligopolies in ocean transport (Hummels, Lugovskyy and Skiba forthcoming), LAC's role as a producer of manufactured goods hinges crucially on improvements in the region's dilapidated transport infrastructure.

Transport costs also play a key role in the region's ability to extract the full benefits of its abundant natural resources. A growing body of evidence suggests that deficiencies in the infrastructure of LAC countries, coupled with a growing congestion of the world logistical chains, have been depriving producers of a substantial part of their profits. This seems to be the case, for instance, of soy producers in western Brazil—discussed in more detail in Chapter 4 of this report—who reportedly spend four times more to ship their product abroad than their counterparts in the U.S. Midwest. Along the same lines, worldwide ship shortages, driven mainly by growing Chinese demand for raw material, have been pushing shipping rates to ever growing heights. The Baltic Dry Index, which reflects freight rates for transporting raw materials, has increased by a factor of 6 since 2001 (as of January 2008) leading to odd situations such as that of iron ore, where ocean shipping these days can be more expensive than the cargo itself.[1]

Transportation is just one of the trade costs not directly linked to trade policy, a category that also includes expenses arising from property rights institutions, regulation and language (Anderson and van Wincoop 2004). A more effective and balanced trade agenda would require actions

[1] The Baltic Dry Index is published by the Baltic Exchange (http://www.balticexchange.com/). See, for instance, Robert Guy Matthews, "Ship Shortages Push Up Prices of Raw Materials," *Wall Street Journal,* October 22, 2007. The article refers to shipments from Brazil to Asia.

to minimize them all. This report, though, focuses on the transport component of those costs and it is particularly concerned about measuring their magnitude and assessing their impact on the volume, composition and direction of LAC's trade.

This focus arises from both pragmatic and analytical reasons. The former are related to the impossibility of obtaining accurate measures of all non-policy components. The latter lie in the growing evidence suggesting that the transport infrastructure is an important constraint on the growth of LAC's trade. Estimates presented in this report suggest that: (a) for most sectors and markets, countries in the region face transport costs that are significantly higher than tariffs; (b) LAC's transport costs tend to be higher than in the developed world, largely because of deficiencies in infrastructure and weak competition in shipping services; (c) although ocean freight expenditures seem to be converging to developed world standards, the opposite seems to be taking place with airfreight; and (d) reductions in freight costs can have a significant and larger impact than tariff liberalization on both volume and diversification of LAC's trade.

As a first approximation, transport costs can be seen as having an impact on trade analogous to that of traditional policy barriers. High transport costs undercut the traditional static gains by limiting specialization and scale, and they also have a negative impact on the so-called dynamic gains insofar as they reduce competition, obstruct knowledge diffusion and increase the costs of introducing new products and penetrating new markets. Yet, given that they are of a different nature, the way they operate and the implications they generate can be fundamentally different from traditional policy barriers.

There are at least three factors that set transport costs apart from other trade costs, particularly tariffs:[2]

(a) Unlike tariffs, transport costs are highly variable over time and the degree of uncertainty is likely to be directly correlated to the quality of the country's infrastructure (quality of the regulation

[2] These points were made by David Hummels in an internal workshop during the preparation of this report.

included). A high degree of uncertainty is likely to inhibit trade, particularly trade of new products, irrespective of the level of transport costs. Given LAC's poor infrastructure, this effect might be playing an important role in holding up export growth and diversification in the region.

(b) Unlike tariffs, transport costs are not a simple, fixed proportion (ad valorem) of the price of products, having a per unit component that has important implications for the composition of the country's exports. Because of this component, transport costs are never product-neutral, bringing higher penalties for products that are more "transport intensive," not only in the sense of having low price-to-weight ratios, but also because of higher time (inventory-holding and depreciation) costs. These are exactly the type of products for which LAC, for its proximity with the U.S. market, enjoys (or should enjoy) both a comparative advantage and a competitive edge.

(c) Unlike tariffs, transport costs are not fixed by fiat, but respond to variables such as trade flows, the quality of the country's infrastructure and the degree of competition in the transport industry. Bringing transport costs down, therefore, goes well beyond the political economy of protection and requires a more complex set of policy actions than those involved in a typical trade liberalization. A particularly thorny issue to deal with is intercountry externalities.

Despite its idiosyncrasies and growing importance in LAC and elsewhere, it was not until recently that trade economists took transport costs more seriously. The tradition was to assume them away with unrealistic assumptions and this deficit of attention has produced a deficit of information. With a few exceptions, governments have devoted few resources to measure and assess the impact of transport costs (and other non-policy trade costs for that matter).

To help fill this knowledge gap and provide more robust information to support policy decisions, this report draws heavily on three major databases that provide a rare insight into the magnitude and impact of transport costs in the region: the Latin American Association of Foreign Trade (ALADI) Foreign Trade Statistics System, the U.S. Census Bureau's Foreign Trade Statistics and the U.S. Department of Transportation's Waterborne Databanks.

ALADI's database reports information on the value and quantity of imports, tariff revenue and transport costs (freight and insurance), disaggregated by "product" (over 5,000 products at the 6-digit level of the Harmonized System classification—"HS"), mode and port of entry for eleven countries (Argentina, Bolivia, Brazil, Chile, Colombia, Ecuador, Mexico, Paraguay, Peru, Uruguay and Venezuela) for 1990 and 1995 and from 2000 to 2005. Not all the information is available for all countries in all years and the most notable missing data is freight rates for Mexico and Venezuela and tariff data for Bolivia, Ecuador, Mexico and Venezuela.

The Census Bureau's database includes information for roughly 17,000 "products" (10-digit level, HS system), on imports (value and weight), tariff revenue, transport costs (freight plus insurance), by mode and district of entry (air and ocean) for all exporters to the United States. The Waterborne Databanks report the same type of information, but limited to ocean shipping, and including information on port of origin and port of entry.[3]

The analysis is organized in six chapters, including this introduction. Chapter 1 reviews the current state of transport costs in the region. It offers some answers to four fundamental questions about LAC's transport costs: (a) how do they compare to tariffs? (b) how do they compare to those elsewhere in the world? (c) what has been their trend? And (d) how "transport-sensitive" are LAC's exports?

Chapter 2 shifts the focus to determinants of transport costs and attempts to isolate the role of a number of complex and interrelated issues ranging from the quality of infrastructure services, to distance, to scale, to market structure. The fundamental question to answer here is: What is behind the level of LAC's transport costs? To shed some light on this issue, this chapter draws on an econometric exercise conducted in a

[3] See the Appendix for more details of the data.

gravity framework, inspired by the most recent contributions of the trade cost literature.

Chapter 3 looks into the relative impact of transport costs and tariffs on the volume and diversification of trade. The aim is to put some hard figures on the claim that LAC should pursue a more balanced trade agenda. It estimates the likely payoffs of reductions in transport costs and further trade liberalization. It seeks to answer questions such as: How much more trade can LAC expect by reducing freight rates? How many more goods can the region expect to export? What would be the impact of an equivalent reduction in tariffs?

Chapter 4 brings the analysis a step closer to the real world. It presents four case studies covering soy in Brazil, farm equipment in Argentina, cotton and textiles in Mexico and cut flowers in Ecuador. These studies look into the logistic chains of those products, present estimates of transport costs and compare them with tariffs and, whenever possible, with the transport costs of competitors. They give an indication of the main factors/bottlenecks behind those costs, among them regulation, the quality of infrastructure and the lack of competition in the transport industry. Chapter 5 presents the conclusions and policy implications.

References

Anderson, J., and E. van Wincoop. 2004. Trade Costs. *Journal of Economic Literature* 42(3): 691–751.

Hummels, David. 2007. Transportation Costs and International Trade in the Second Era of Globalization. *Journal of Economic Perspectives* 21(3): 131–54.

Hummels, D., V. Lugovskyy and A. Skiba. Forthcoming. The Trade Reducing Effects of Market Power in International Shipping. *Journal of Development Economics.*

IDB (Inter-American Development Bank). 2006. *The Emergence of China. Opportunities and Challenges for Latin America and the Caribbean,* ed. Robert Devlin, Antoni Estevadeordal and Andrés Rodríguez-Clare. Washington, D.C.: IDB and Cambridge, MA: David Rockefeller Center for Latin American Studies, Harvard University.

Chapter 1

An Overview of Trade and Transport Costs in LAC

Tariffs have come down substantially in the region—with MFN tariffs falling from an average of more than 40 percent in the mid 1980s to close to 10 percent in the late 1990s and preferential tariffs falling even further (IDB 2002)—and, arguably, the world has never been so closely integrated and yet, the discussion on policy-related trade costs still dominates the trade agenda in LAC. Does that still accurately reflect the predominance of traditional trade barriers over other forms of trade costs? A quick, back-of-the-envelope calculation taking into account the extent of the unilateral trade liberalizations and the trade agreements recently implemented suggests that the answer is no. But how exactly do these traditional barriers compare with other trade costs, such as freight expenditures?

If policy makers are going to revise the trade agenda, and that is one of the main points of this report, they need more than back-of-the-envelope calculations. This chapter draws on detailed quantitative information to put together a first approximation of the level of LAC's transport costs and their relevance to trade. It begins by shedding some light on their importance vis-à-vis tariff barriers and on how they fare compared to the levels seen in other regions of the world. It then moves on to assess how LAC's transport costs have evolved in the last decade and how "transport-intensive" (both in terms of time and freight) LAC's exports are.

Transport Costs versus Tariffs

Figure 1.1 gives a broad picture of the relative magnitude of transport costs and tariffs for both intra- and extraregional imports.[4] On the vertical axis we

[4] The concept of transport costs used here covers only freight expenditures involved in bringing the good from alongside the carrier at the port of exportation in the country of exportation and placing it alongside the first port of entry in the importer country. It does not include insurance.

Figure 1.1. Ad Valorem Freight and Real Tariffs for Intra- and Extraregional Imports, Selected LAC Countries, 2005

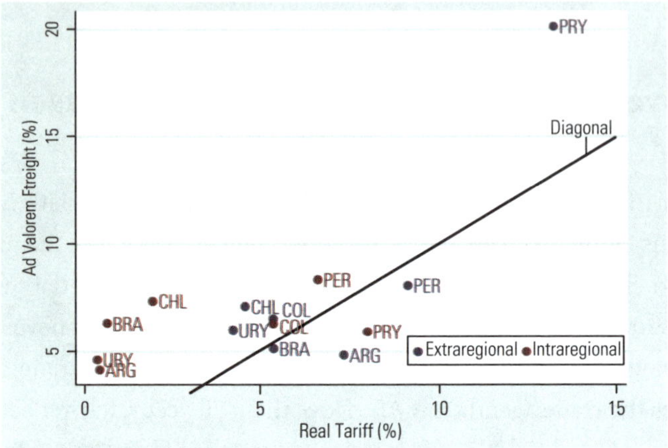

Note: Freight is the ratio of freight expenditures to imports. Real tariffs is the ratio of tariff revenue to imports. Tariff data for Paraguay and Colombia are for 2000 and 2003, respectively. See Table 1.A.1 for data.

Source: Author's calculation based on ALADI Data.

measure the ad valorem freight rate and on the horizontal axis we measure the ad valorem tariff on imports calculated as tariff revenue divided by the value of imports. We plot both intra- and extraregional freights and tariffs and countries that are on the left of the graph diagonal have average (weighted) freight rates that are higher than average (weighted) tariffs. It is clear that when it comes to trade within the region, all countries in the sample, with the exception of Paraguay, are on the left of the diagonal. That is, transport costs, which range from 4 percent in Argentina to 8 percent in Peru, are higher than tariffs by a large margin. For extraregional trade, the picture is mixed, with three countries—Argentina, Brazil and Peru—having higher tariffs than freight costs (and therefore being positioned at the right side of the diagonal). However, even in this group, the tariff difference to freight costs (that is, the distance to the diagonal) is too small to justify a trade agenda focused primarily on policy barriers. Extraregional freight rates range from 5 percent in Argentina to as much as 20 percent in landlocked Paraguay. As expected, Paraguay seems to pay a high price for not having access to sea.

It is also worth noting that despite the obvious differences in proximity, the average cost of shipping goods intraregionally is not that much different from shipping goods abroad, with the exception, again, of Paraguay. In some cases, such as Brazil, Chile and Peru, the former exceeds the latter. Moreover, estimates in Figure 1.1 are trade-weighted averages and, as such, they tend to underestimate transport and tariff costs since trade flows already reflect the attempt by exporters and importers to trade goods with the lowest trade costs. Simple averages are much higher for both freights and tariffs, with intraregional freights ranging from 6.5 percent in Argentina to 12 percent in Colombia and extraregional freights ranging from 7.5 percent in Uruguay to a particularly punitive 25 percent in Paraguay. The story, though, about the dominance of freight over tariffs remains valid in intraregional trade, and changes slightly when it comes to trading abroad.[5]

Figure 1.2 also looks at trade costs, but from the perspective of LAC's exports rather than imports. Since the product and market compositions of these two flows are markedly different, export data could tell a different story.[6] Unfortunately, data on trade costs for exports is only available for the United States and five Latin American markets.[7] It is clear that the dominance of freight over tariff is even more pronounced, with all countries positioned to the left of the diagonal, except for intraregional exports of Ecuador and Uruguay's exports to the United States.

Unlike the result for imports, though, LAC's freights to the United States are markedly higher than intraregional freights, except for the case of landlocked Bolivia (exports of gas via pipeline to Brazil explain this result), Mexico (proximity rules!) and Venezuela, where the reverse is true. It is also

---

[5] Argentina remains in the group with tariffs higher than freights, now joined by Uruguay. In the other countries, freights dominate by a small margin, with the exception of Chile, where the difference is substantial. The point made earlier about the similarity of intra- and extraregional freight remains valid, with the exception, again, of Paraguay. See Table 1.A.1 for data.

[6] In most LAC countries, natural resource-based products have a much bigger weight in extraregional exports than imports. That is not always the case in intraregional trade.

[7] Neither Europe nor Asia collects data on FOB imports, making it impossible to get estimates of transport costs of LAC's exports to those markets.

Figure 1.2. Ad Valorem Freight and Real Tariffs for Intraregional Exports and Exports to the U.S. Selected LAC Countries. 2005

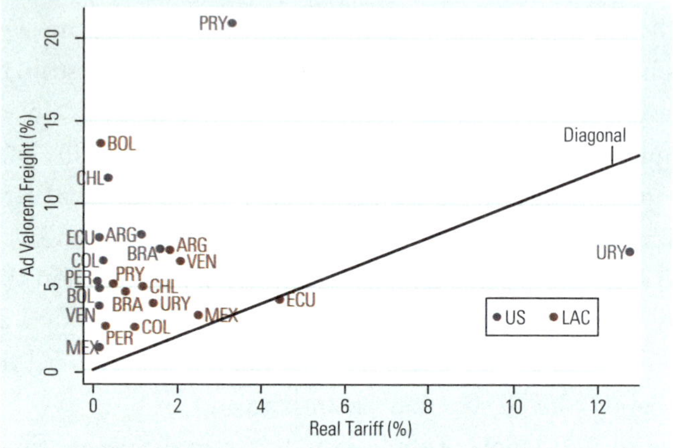

Note: Graph is based on import data from export markets. Freight is the ratio of freight expenditures to imports. Real tariffs is the ratio of tariff revenue to imports. Intraregional exports include Brazil, Argentina, Chile, Peru and Uruguay. See Table 1.A.2 in the Appendix for the raw data.

Source: Author's calculation based on U.S. Census Bureau and ALADI data.

interesting to note that geography does not always prevail in explaining the differences in shipping costs to the United States. This is clearly the case of Ecuador and, less so, Colombia, which have freight costs comparable to those of the countries in the Southern Cone. Whether this is due to differences in the composition of goods exported or in the quality of the infrastructure is something we investigate in more detail in the next chapter. As in the case of imports, simple averages point to substantially higher tariff and freight costs than weighted averages, but do not change the story about the dominance of freight over tariffs (see Table 1.A.2 in the Appendix).

We have established so far that on average transport costs are higher than tariffs, but what does this imply? How do we translate these findings in terms of volume and composition of trade? How much does the region stand to gain by giving transport at least the same kind of attention it has given so far to tariffs? In Chapter 3, we take this story about the dominance of transport costs over tariffs one step further and try to assess its economic significance.

How Do LAC's Transport Costs Compare Abroad?

Figures 1.1 and 1.2 reveal how transport costs vary within the region according to the flow and direction of trade, but do not provide any information on how these costs compare with those of other countries and regions around the world. Judging by the (scattered) evidence available on the quality of LAC's transport infrastructure, it seems likely that freight costs in the region are considerably higher than in developed countries and higher even than in other emerging regions such as Asia. Traditional indicators such as the percentage of roads paved, port transit times or qualitative indicators based on perceptions, all suggest that LAC's infrastructure, with a few exceptions, lags behind other developing and developed regions of the world.

For instance, according to the *Global Competitiveness Report 2007–2008* (World Economic Forum 2007), only three Latin American and Caribbean countries are placed among the top half of the ranking in the Infrastructure Pillar, namely Chile (31), Panama (50) and El Salvador (61). The *Doing Business 2008* (World Bank 2007a) places LAC well behind the global best practice for trading across borders. According to the survey, the region takes, on average, twice the number of days to export than the high-income economies of the Organisation for Economic Co-operation and Development (OECD). According to the World Bank's (2007b) *Connecting to Compete* Report of 2007, the Latin American region is still logistically constrained, facing many challenges ranging from high transport costs to poor infrastructure and customs performance to poor reliability of the trading system. But how bad is it exactly? How much more does the region pay to transport its goods? What are the actual figures?

It is not easy to give definite answers to these questions because there are not many countries in the world that collect data on international trade freights, let alone on domestic freight rates. The United States is one of the few exceptions and provides a rare opportunity to get some international perspective on LAC's freight costs.

Looking at imports—Figure 1.3 combines the U.S. Census Bureau's with ALADI's data and suggests that LAC spends nearly twice as much as the United States to import its goods, with Argentina presenting the lowest

Figure 1.3. Total Import Freight Expenditures as a Share of Imports, U.S. and Selected LAC Countries, 2005 (%)

	US	ARG	BRA	URY	COL	LAC	CHL	PER	PRY
%	3.7	5.1	5.5	5.7	6.7	7.2	7.5	8.5	15

Note: Latin America (LAC) is the simple average of Paraguay (PRY), Peru (PER), Chile (CHL), Colombia (COL), Brazil (BRA), Uruguay (URY) and Argentina (ARG). Freight expenditures include freight and insurance.

Source: Author's calculations based on ALADI and U.S. Census Bureau data.

costs (22 percent above the United States) and Paraguay, the highest (3.5 times the U.S. level).

LAC's higher transport costs may be driven by differences in the composition of its trade (with whom it trades, what it trades and how it ships its goods) and by inefficiencies in its infrastructure, including issues of scale, competition and regulation. These distinctions matter for designing optimal policy responses, but whatever the relative importance of these factors, we can, at the very least, argue that LAC pays a lot more to transport its goods and, therefore, governments should be paying a lot more attention to transport costs when formulating their trade policy than they have done so far.

In Chapter 2, we use econometrics to provide a better grasp of the relative importance of the roles played by trade composition and infrastructure. Here, we just try to stimulate the discussion by comparing freight expenditures across modes of transportation, categories of goods and neighboring countries. Table 1.1 reveals LAC's transport mode composition and that of the United States. In the case of the former, the modal composition of

Table 1.1. Transport Mode Composition of Imports

Selected LAC Countries and U.S., 2005 (%)

	From All Countries				From LAC			
Country	Air	Maritime	Land	Others**	Air	Maritime	Land	Others
Brazil	24.6	67.5	5.8	2.1	4.0	51.3	37.5	7.2
Colombia	27.9	59.0	8.8	4.3	18.6	61.1	16.9	3.4
Argentina	17.2	52.9	23.6	6.3	10.6	43.1	43.8	2.5
Bolivia	14.4	0	80.6	5.0	6.7	0	86.9	6.4
Chile	13.5	65.7	15.7	5.1	7.3	42.1	37.5	13.1
Ecuador	16.5	73.6	8.9	1.0	11.1	65.8	18.4	4.7
Mexico	8.2	20.5	55.0	16.3	5.3	66.4	12.9	15.4
Peru	13.8	82.1	3.7	0.4	6.6	86.0	6.9	0.5
Paraguay	10.7	0	45.8	43.5	2.4	0	77.0	20.6
Uruguay	7.9	49.4	25.7	17.0	4.1	21.6	46.6	27.7
Venezuela	19.6	70.9	9.4	0.1	14.1	59.8	26.0	0.1
LAC*	15.8	49.2	25.7	9.2	8.3	45.2	37.3	9.2
U.S.	21.6	51.6	26.7			—		

Note: Data for Argentina and Bolivia is for 2004.
* Simple average.
** Includes river, lake, mail shipments and pipelines.

Source: Author's calculation based on ALADI data and U.S. Census Bureau data.

intraregional trade is also included. It is clear that there is substantial variance both within LAC and between LAC and the United States. Countries such as Brazil, Colombia, Argentina and Venezuela have profiles similar to that of the United States, with airplanes playing a significant role, whereas Mexico, Paraguay and Bolivia are a quite different story, with a clear dominance of land transportation. A different story emerges when we look at intraregional trade, with land transportation assuming a prominent role in most countries except for Peru.

Modal composition reflects not only exogenous factors such as geography, but also direct or indirect policy decisions that can ultimately facilitate or hamper the choice of a transport mix that minimizes freight costs. Some analysts argue that LAC's policy choices in transport have been more a hindrance than help. Batista da Silva (1996, p. 19), for instance, argues "in emphasizing roads over rail, river and coastal logistics systems, these countries have selected the most expensive as well as the least environmental friendly option for their infrastructure system." There is some data corroborating this stance, particularly in the case of Brazil, with a World Bank report arguing that avoidable logistic costs by means of a more cost-effective use of multimodal transport, "were adding more than US$1.2 billion per year to the costs of external trade and at least US$1.3 billion per year to the costs of domestic interregional trade in corridors with available rail services" (World Bank 2004, p. 18).

These differences in the modal mix are compounded by differences in the goods composition of trade across countries, so to make this benchmark more meaningful, Figure 1.4 compares air and ocean freight costs across product categories for the United States and selected LAC countries.[8] On the vertical axis, we measure ad valorem ocean freight and on the horizontal axis we measure ad valorem airfreight. We plot a reference line through the U.S. levels, so that we can easily compare LAC freight levels with that of the United States. For instance, countries that are in the northeast (southwest) quadrant have both ocean and airfreight rates that are higher (lower) than those of the United States.

The picture that emerges still points to lower costs in the United States (most LAC countries in most categories are in the northeast quadrant), but with some nuances. In the case of airfreight, the United States comes out with lower costs than all LAC countries in all categories of goods. In ocean freight, the gap with the United States is generally smaller and in some cases, such as Argentina, Brazil and Uruguay in agriculture, Argentina and Brazil in manufacturing and Chile in mining, it is either minimal or favors the LAC countries.

Another all-important dimension that affects these results is the distance between trade partners (partner composition). Countries that are more isolated are likely to have higher transport costs no matter how developed and efficient their infrastructure is. Short of a full econometric exercise, one way of looking at this is to take into account how costly it is for these countries to trade with their neighbors. Of course,

[8] Even though data on land freight is available from both ALADI and the U.S. Department of Transportation TransBorder Surface Freight Dataset, it is hard to interpret since there is no information on the distances involved.

Figure 1.4. Total Air and Ocean Freight Expenditure as a Share of Imports. U.S. versus Selected LAC Countries by Mode and Category of Goods. 2005

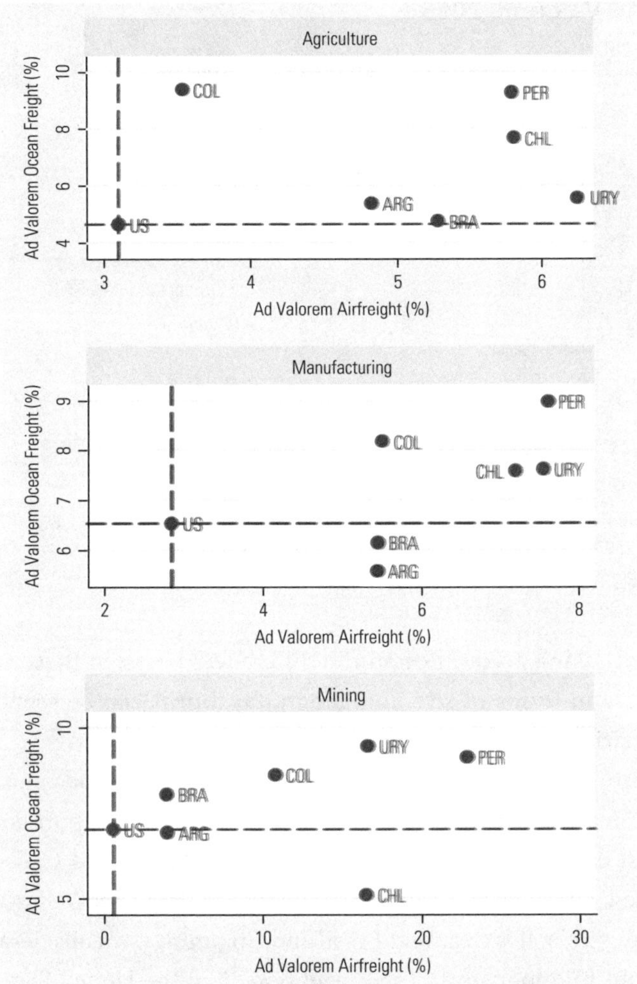

Note: Freight includes insurance. Goods categories follow WTO-SITC classification. Countries: Peru (PER), Argentina (ARG), Brazil (BRA), Uruguay (URY), Colombia (COL) and Chile (CHL).

Source: U.S. Census Bureau and ALADI.

Figure 1.5. Trading with Neighbors: Ocean and Airfreight Import Expenditures. U.S. versus Selected LAC Countries by Category of Goods. Ad Valorem, 2005

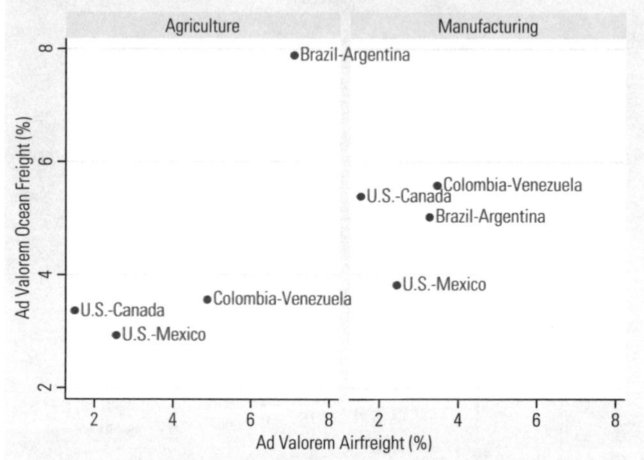

Note: Goods categories follow WTO-SITC classification. Freight expenditures include insurance.

Source: Author's calculation based on ALADI and U.S. Census Bureau data.

we are not taking account of all the differences between these countries, particularly in terms of size and geography, but it can be seen as a first approximation.

Figure 1.5 reveals how costly it is, by category of goods and mode of transport, for the United States, Brazil and Colombia to import goods from their most economically important neighbors: Mexico and Canada in the case of the United States, Argentina in the case of Brazil and Venezuela in the case of Colombia. It is clear that Brazil and Colombia pay considerably more in airfreight to import from their neighbors than the United States, particularly in agriculture. In ocean freight, there are more nuances, with Brazil paying nearly five times more to import agricultural goods from Argentina than the United States pays to import from Canada, whereas Colombia's cost disadvantages in its trade with Venezuela seem small. In the case of manufacturing, differences in freight expenditures for both Brazil and Colombia are only significant with respect to U.S. trade with Mexico.

Looking at exports—So far we have compared LAC's levels of transport costs by looking just at imports. As argued before, freight expenditures to export may tell a different story since we are looking at a considerably different set of goods, modes and partners. Since data on export freights is available only for a limited number of markets and countries in LAC and is not available for the United States, we use U.S. import data to compare LAC's levels with those of other exporters to the United States.

As with import freights, differences in the goods composition of trade and in the distance to the United States make it difficult to draw definitive conclusions just by looking at the raw data alone. Yet, this type of data does give us some food for thought. For instance, Figures 1.6a and 1.6b compare the ad valorem freight rates of a number of LAC countries with that of China, Oceania (Australia and New Zealand), East Asia (Japan, Korea and Taiwan) and of a group of 12 European countries (EU-12).[9] The comparison is done by mode and goods category.

It is immediately obvious that proximity does not always translate into lower freight rates. In ocean freight this is particularly clear with agricultural goods, where most LAC countries have higher rates than countries in the Far East and in Europe. In manufacturing, we see most of Central America and some countries in the Caribbean occupying the low end of the rate spectrum, but with rates that are not that much different from those of the EU-12 or East Asia. On the higher end, we see, as expected, most of South America, but some Caribbean countries as well. Note that most of them have either higher or similar rates to those of China and Oceania. The picture in mining is more mixed, but again we see countries that are very close to the United States, such as Mexico and Ecuador, with freight rates that are higher than far away China or Oceania.

In airfreight, we focus on manufacturing and agriculture since airplanes do not play a significant role in the transportation of mining products. What we see is a pattern similar to ocean freight, but the lack of correlation between LAC's proximity and its freight rates is even starker.

[9] The EU-12 are Belgium, Germany, Denmark, Spain, France, U.K., Greece, Ireland, Italy, Luxemburg, Netherlands, and Portugal.

Figure 1.6a. Ocean Freight Expenditures as a Share of Exports to the U.S. LAC and Selected Regions. 2006

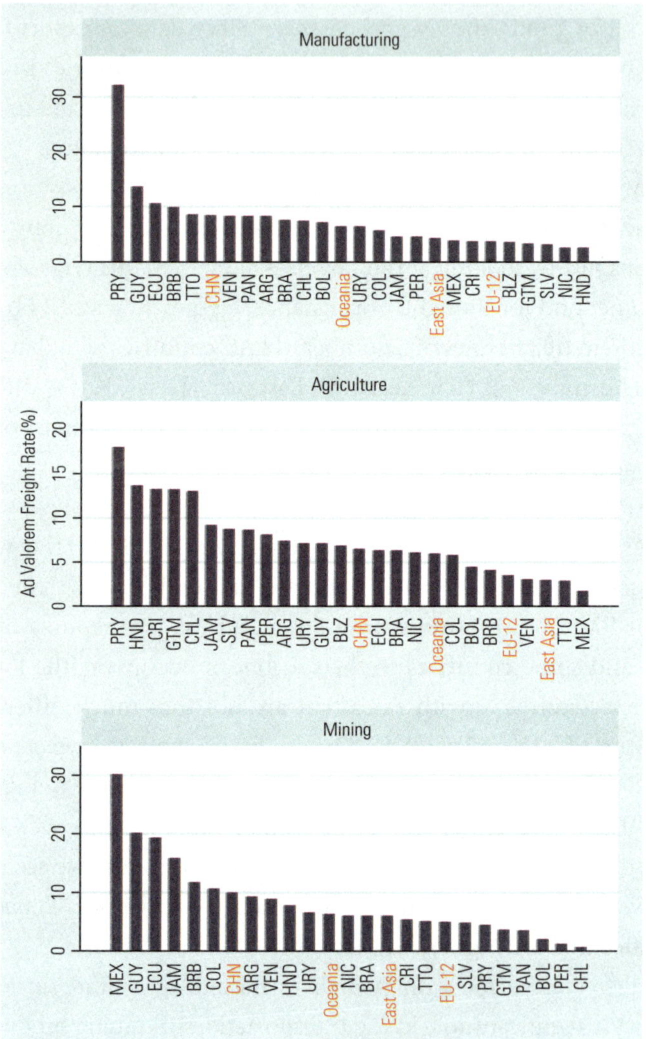

Note: Goods categories follow WTO-SITC classification.
Freight includes insurance. See appendix for region groups.
Source: U.S. Census Bureau.

There is little doubt that these results reflect differences in the composition of goods (as we will see below LAC exports heavier products than Asia or Europe) and the quality of the infrastructure, among other factors. As with imports, in Chapter 2 we dig deeper into this issue, looking at the

Figure 1.6b. Airfreight Expenditures as a Share of Exports to the U.S. LAC and Selected Regions. 2006

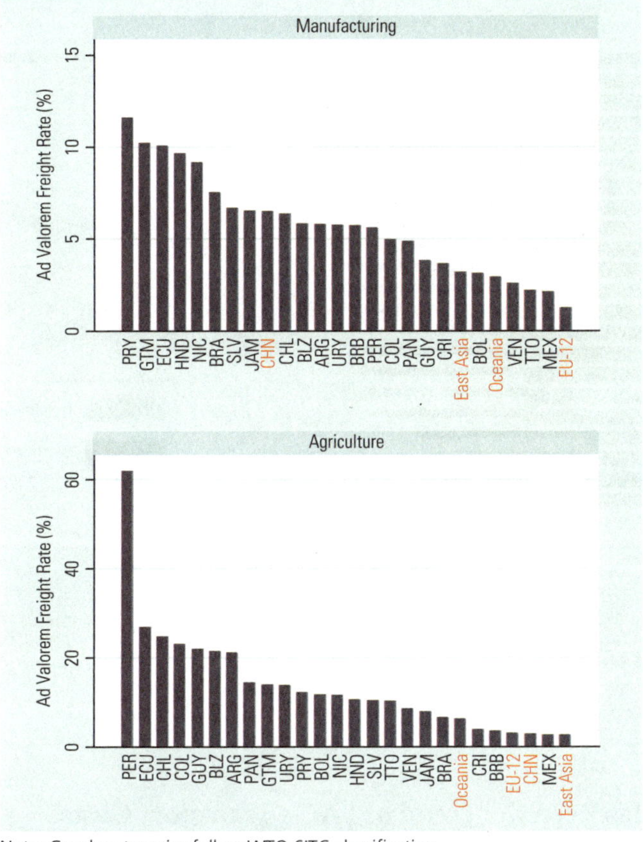

Note: Goods categories follow WTO-SITC classification.
Freight includes insurance. See appendix for region groups.
Source: U.S. Census Bureau.

determinants of freight rates with a more refined methodology and with more disaggregated data. But for now, a simple exercise comparing LAC's and China's export freight rates of similar "products" (10-digit HS level) to the United States seems like a useful step towards uncovering what is behind LAC's freight rates. As can be seen in Figure 1.6c, even when we compare freight by matching products with a very high level of disaggregation, LAC's freight rates are far from reflecting the proximity advantage the region has in exporting to the United States. In the case of Ecuador, the average ad valorem freight rate is even higher than that of China.

Figure 1.6c. Ratios between LAC's and China's Export Freight and Distance to the U.S. Manufactured Goods, All Modes, 2006

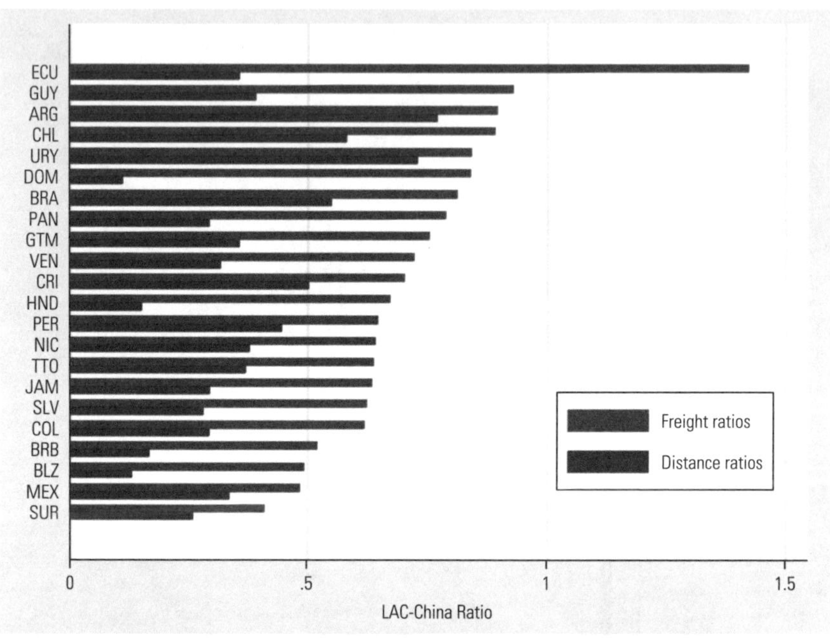

Note: Freight ratios are based on simple average ad valorem freight rates of similar products (10-digit HS). Distance ratios are based on the average distance between the U.S. and the countries' main ports. Manufacturing defined as in the WTO-SITC classification.

Source: U.S. Census Bureau.

What Has Been the Trend of LAC's Transport Costs?

LAC's transport costs seem to be relatively high, but what has been the recent trend? Are they converging to developed country levels? Are things getting worse or can we already see signs of improvement? As with levels, comparisons of transport cost trends across countries are difficult because the composition of the countries' trade (what and with whom they trade) changes over time. So, just by looking at the raw data it is hard to tell if a country's transport costs are going up (down) because of a deterioration (improvement) of its infrastructure or because it began to trade heavier (lighter) goods to further off (nearer) countries. As mentioned before, this distinction is important if the objective is to design effective public policies.

To make this distinction clear, we resort to a simple econometric model that, by regressing ad valorem freight on the traded goods'

Figure 1.7. Trend in Import Airfreight after Controlling for Changes in Trade Composition, U.S. and Selected LAC Countries, 1995–2005. 1995 = 100

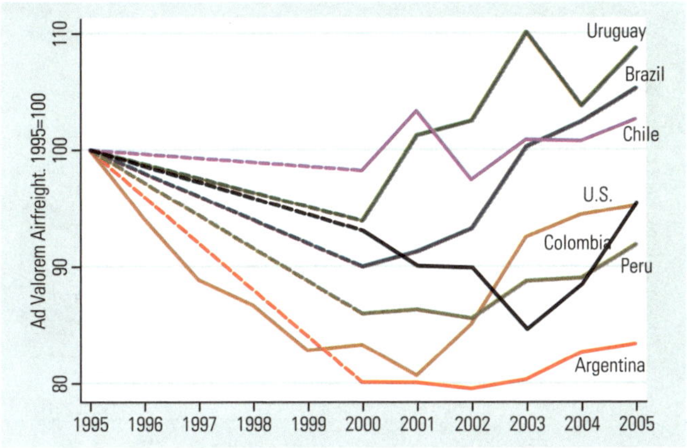

Note: Airfreight is freight plus insurance as a share of imports. It was estimated by regressing ad valorem freight on the weight-to-value ratio of the goods imported and on year and partner-good fixed effects. Data for LAC countries is only available for 1995 and 2000–2005. See text for details.

Source: ALADI and U.S. Census Bureau.

weight-to-value ratio and on year and commodity-partner dummies, allows us to net out the impact of changes in trade composition.[10] As before, we look at both import and export freights, focusing on transport modes and countries for which there is data available.

Figures 1.7 and 1.8 present the estimated trends in import air and ocean freights, respectively, for a number of LAC countries and the United States. What we see in the pictures are trends represented by indices (1995 = 100), net of compositional changes, which are driven not only by infrastructure-related events, including factors such as scale and regulation, but also by another key determinant of freight expenditures: fuel costs. Since we are only interested in the former and the latter is an international commodity, whose prices can be reasonably assumed to be shared by all countries, what matters is the countries' relative trend, particularly, LAC's trend with respect to the United States.

The results for airfreight are not good news for LAC, except for Argentina and to a lesser extent Peru. For most countries in the sample, the trend in airfreight is U-shaped, with costs falling until the late 1990s, a period in which

[10] The model follows Hummels (2007a). See Appendix 1.B.1 for model specification and results.

Figure 1.8. Trend in Import Ocean Freight after Controlling for Changes in Trade Composition, U.S. and Selected LAC Countries, 1995–2005. 1995 = 100

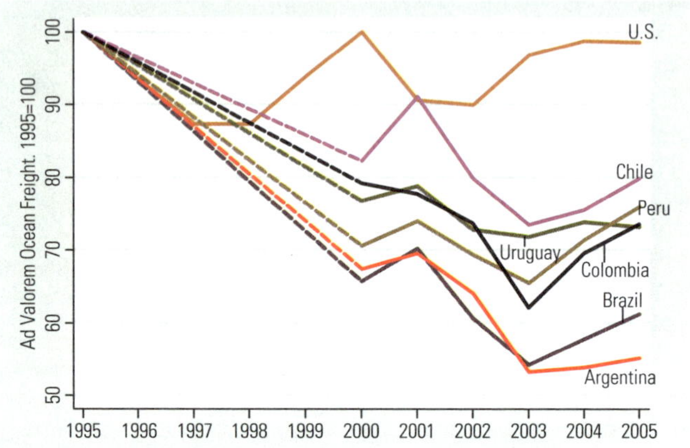

Note: Ocean freight is freight plus insurance as a share of imports. It was estimated by regressing ad valorem freight on the weight-to-value ratio of the goods imported and on year and partner-good fixed effects. Data for LAC countries is only available for 1995 and 2000–2005. See text for details.

Source: ALADI and U.S. Census Bureau.

oil prices were roughly stable, and shooting up after that, in tandem with the hike in oil prices. However, the drop in airfreight was much more significant in the United States than in LAC countries, except for Argentina. When costs started to climb in the 2000s, LAC countries' costs increased roughly at the same pace as the United States, with the exception of Argentina and Peru. Overall, what we see in the last decade is that countries such as Uruguay, Brazil and Chile had their costs moving further away from the lower U. S. levels. In Colombia, the gap remained roughly the same, whereas we see some convergence in Peru and Argentina, particularly in the latter.

In ocean freight (Figure 1.8), the picture is much brighter, with all the countries in the sample showing substantial reductions in their expenditures over the period—particularly in Brazil and Argentina—whereas U.S. costs remained roughly stable. From 2003 onwards, though, there are some preliminary but worrying signs of a reversal in the process of convergence, which can only be confirmed once more recent data is available.

Figures 1.9 and 1.10 look at the export side of LAC's freight expenditures, using U.S. import data. The trend in LAC's export freights, grouped

Figure 1.9. Trend in Export Airfreight to the U.S. after Controlling for Trade Composition, Selected LAC Subregions, China and the Rest of the World (ROW), 1994–2006. 1994 = 100

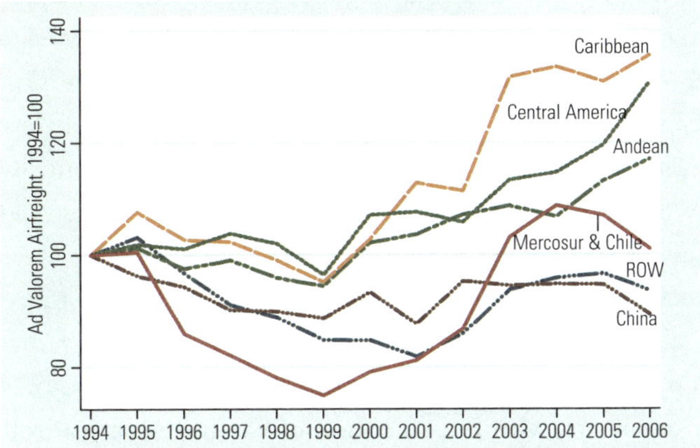

Note: Airfreight is freight plus insurance as a share of imports. It was estimated by regressing ad valorem freight on the weight-to-value ratio of the goods imported and on year and partner-good fixed effects. See text for details.

Source: U.S. Census Bureau.

Figure 1.10. Trend in Export Ocean Freight to the U.S. after Controlling for Trade Composition, Selected LAC Subregions, China and the Rest of the World (ROW), 1994–2006. 1994 = 100

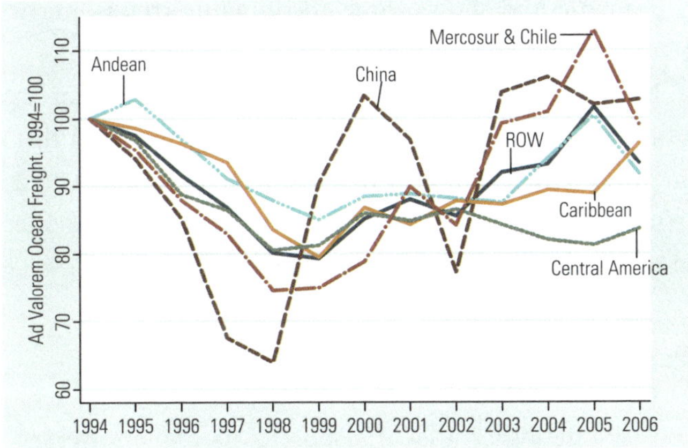

Note: Ocean freight is freight plus insurance as a share of imports. It was estimated by regressing ad valorem freight on the weight-to-value ratio of the goods imported and on year and partner-good fixed effects. See text for details.

Source: U.S. Census Bureau.

by subregions for presentation purposes, is compared against China and the rest of the world's exporters to the United States. As with imports, the results for air and ocean freights suggest two radically different scenarios. In air, we see freight expenditures in LAC diverging sharply from other U.S. exporters, particularly China, to the point where freights in 2006 were well above the 1995 level—by as much as 36 percent in subregions such as the Caribbean—whereas China and the other exporters managed to keep costs below the 1995 mark, despite the oil shock. True, Mercosur and Chile had much better performances than other LAC subregions, but the exceptional gains of the 1990s were rapidly reversed in the 2000s.

In ocean freight, once again, the results are much more positive for LAC, although we do not see the type of gains observed in import freights. Overall most subregions follow closely the changes in costs affecting other exporters, with the exception of Central America in the 2000s, when the subregion managed to reduce costs while they were increasing everywhere else.

Altogether, the combination of relatively high freight costs with increasing and diverging trends suggests that air transportation, for both imports and exports, is probably the most troublesome link in the region's international logistic chain and, therefore, where the potential to reduce trade costs is probably at its peak. The situation in ocean freight clearly looks less dramatic and shows some encouraging trends, particularly on the import side.

The burning question behind all this data is, what exactly has been driving those results? Chapter 2 makes an attempt in this direction by focusing on the determinants of transport costs. It is a first step in a research effort that has necessarily to involve a lot of country-specific work to take into account the diversity of the situations in the region.

How "Transport-Sensitive" Are LAC's Exports?

We have so far established that transport costs are, on average, a higher obstacle to LAC's trade than tariffs. We have also seen that the region, with a few exceptions, spends proportionally more to transport the goods it trades than the United States, Europe and Asia. Finally, we have seen that trends in LAC's transport costs bring mixed news in terms of convergence to developed world levels.

As comprehensive as this body of evidence is, it overlooks two important and deeply intertwined dimensions, which are key to a better understanding of the strategic importance of transport costs to the region: the idiosyncrasies of the region's comparative advantage and the time costs of transportation.

Whatever the level and trend of its transport costs, the characteristics and requirements of LAC's comparative advantages carry enough weight (literally) to put them among the very top public policy priorities. In a world market increasingly crowded by vast, extremely labor-abundant and resource-scarce countries, LAC's economic future seems to be inexorably tied, first, to the exploitation of natural resources (raw and otherwise) and, second, to taking advantage of its proximity to the world's largest markets.

Natural resources—As is well known, the exploitation of natural resources has a vast logistical component that figures among its most important, if not the most important, variable costs. Executives at CVRD, the Brazilian company that is the world's largest exporter of iron ore, typically mention logistics as their core business. We do not have to go far to understand why. Grains, minerals and commodities in general are very "heavy" products to the extent that they have very high weight-to-value ratios: a dollar's worth of iron ore exports is many times heavier than a dollar's worth of semiconductors.

Since freight costs have been shown to be directly proportional to weight-to-value ratios (Hummels 2001), natural resources exporters pay relatively more to transport their goods. The implication of this simple relationship is not hard to grasp: just as a poor logistic chain can eat away profits from companies such as CRVD, a poor and costly transport infrastructure can severely undercut the rents that whole countries can extract from their natural resources, transferring income from producers to monopolistic and inefficient "freight-forwarders" or ports, roads and airport operators. Rents can also be hurt by the (costly) damage that a poor infrastructure can cause to the quality of the goods exported. To put it simply, natural resource exporters, by the very physical characteristics of their products, are condemned to have their transport infrastructure at the top of their public policy priorities. To do otherwise is to risk wasting some of the country's most valuable resources.

Proximity—The issue with proximity goes beyond natural resources and part of it involves the second overlooked dimension of our analysis so far: time costs. We know for a fact that freight costs are determined not only by weight-to-value ratios, but also by distance. Our own estimates presented in Chapter 2, using U.S. and LAC data (Tables 2.B.3 and 2.B.4), suggest that an increase of 10 percent in distance raises freight expenditure, on average, by 1.7 percent for air and by 1.8 percent for ocean shipping. This proximity edge can be particularly sizeable in high weight-to-value goods, since we are considering savings that are applied to goods that carry proportionally higher transport costs.

We can then safely argue that producers positioned closer to markets can potentially use these savings in transport costs to make up for disadvantages in labor or capital costs (or for any other cost disadvantage for that matter) that they have with regard to producers in more distant countries. In other words, when it comes to its own internal market, the U.S. market and, to a lesser extent, the European market, LAC has a "natural" transport cost advantage over low-labor-cost producers in Asia, particularly in "heavy goods." These include not only natural resources, but also "heavy" manufactured goods such as agricultural machinery, heavy construction equipment and even "high-tech" goods such as large plasma TVs.

Figure 1.11 illustrates the two points made so far, using data for the U.S. market. It is clear that for most LAC subregions the average weight of their exports is (considerably) higher than East Asia's and also higher than the average of other exporters (excluding LAC, Canada and East Asia) to the United States. This is driven mainly by natural resources, but it is also a characteristic shared by manufactured goods exported by most of the region. Proximity, therefore, does seem to have an influence in LAC's pattern of exports to the United States, shifting it towards "heavy," transport-intensive goods (in the sense of having intrinsically higher ad valorem freights), even if we are not talking about natural resources. This is in line with a point

Figure 1.11. Weight per US$ Exported to the U.S., LAC and Other Exporters, 2006. kg per US$

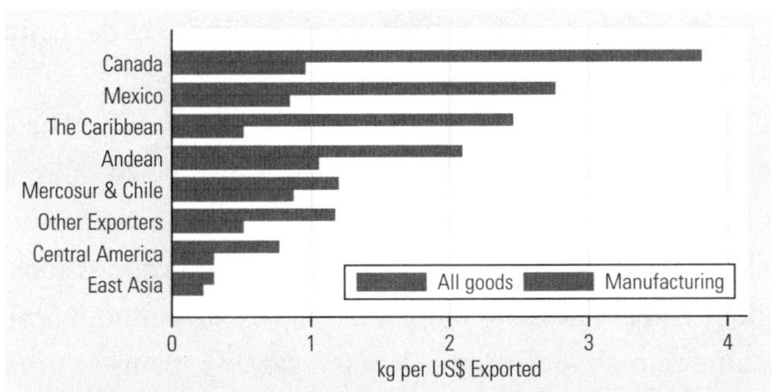

Note: Weight-to-value ratios are country weighted averages (export value) of goods shipped by air and ocean. Figures for subregions are simple averages of the countries' ratios. East Asia includes Japan, China, Hong Kong, Taiwan, Macau and Korea.

Source: U.S. Census Bureau.

made by Harrigan (2005) that the combination of proximity (distance) and the physical characteristics of the products plays a significant role in the countries' pattern of trade.

Proximity, though, is not only about the geographical distance between countries, but also about the time taken to cover this distance. Poorly maintained roads, congested airports, inefficient ports and dysfunctional customs services can waste away the advantages of being geographically close by overly increasing shipping times. Some of the costs of longer shipping times are reflected in freight expenditures since they translate into higher personnel (more people working longer hours) and equipment costs (faster depreciation due to poor conditions and lower utilization rates, i.e. fewer trips per piece of equipment), but some key others, such as the higher depreciation and inventory costs of the goods being traded, are not. To have, then, a complete picture of the state of LAC transport costs, we would need to factor in transit times and the extra costs they may or may not impose when compared to other regions in the world. We would also have to look at freight costs and times within borders.

Data constraints put this task beyond the reach of this report, but keeping track of time costs is key for policy makers in the region for at least two good reasons: it can erode LAC's advantage in "heavy goods" as discussed earlier, but it can also undermine LAC's comparative and competitive advantages in exporting "time-sensitive" goods to the United States, to the region and even to the world.

The time factor—What are "time-sensitive goods"? The literature speaks of goods whose costs are extremely sensitive to shipping times because of an accelerated depreciation, driven, on the supply side, by the physical characteristics of the product (e.g. perishable goods such as fruits, fresh produce and cut flowers) or by the fast pace of technological progress (e.g. semiconductors); and, on the demand side, by stringent time requirements (e.g. inputs to just-in-time assembly) or by unpredictability and volatility of the customers' preferences (e.g. holiday toys and high fashion apparel) (Hummels 2001).

Even though we can come up with a more or less precise definition of what these goods are, to clearly identify a set of goods is a more complicated story. The rapid pace of change in product and process technologies, the increasing fragmentation of the world production, the ever-growing customer preference for timely delivery and the significant drop in airfreight over the last decades (Hummels 2007a, Harrigan 2005) all conspire to increase demand for timeliness and to constantly change product sensitivity to shipping times.

With this ever-changing set of time-sensitive goods, can we say something about their importance to LAC's exports? As a first approximation, we can easily cite a number of anecdotes that suggest that they are far from marginal and in many instances are among the countries' most important exports. The cases range from fruits and salmon in Chile, to fashion apparel and semiconductors in Central America, to dairy products in Argentina and Uruguay, to cut flowers in Colombia and Ecuador (reviewed in detail in Chapter 4), to asparagus in Peru and auto parts and apparel in Mexico. We can also resort to the literature, where we see findings such as Evans and Harrigan's (2005), which point to a shift during the 1990s in the sourcing of U.S. apparel toward Mexico and the Caribbean, "disproportionately concentrated in goods where timeliness is important" (p. 293).

Figure 1.12. Ad Valorem per Day Time Cost of Exports to the U.S. LAC and Other Exporters. Trade Weighted, 2000–2006 Average

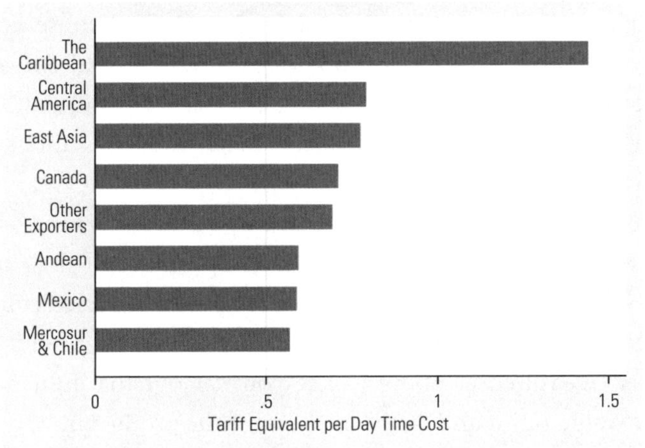

Note: Figures for subregions are simple averages of the countries' ratios. East Asia includes Japan, China, Hong Kong,Taiwan, Macau and Korea.

Source: Author's calculation based on data from Hummels and Schaur (2007) and U.S. Census Bureau.

To try to go beyond anecdotes and case studies, we use a general indicator of time sensitiveness or product timeliness developed by Hummels and Schaur (2007), which uses a sophisticated econometric model to capture product-specific time costs. The indicator—tariff equivalent of time saving per day—reflects the premium for air shipping that firms are willing to pay to avoid an additional day of ocean transport. It balances the benefits of delivering goods faster, measured in terms of days, against the higher monetary shipping costs. As the name suggests, the time costs are measured just as ad valorem tariffs, that is, as a percentage of the price of the product, and is estimated at a fine level of disaggregation, based on U.S. merchandise import data from 1991–2005.[11]

In Figure 1.12, we use this product-level indicator to calculate the average time cost per day of the region's exports to the United States for 2000–2006, having the share of each product in the export basket as

[11] 4-digit of Harmonized System.

weights.[12] As can be seen, export time costs vary widely across the region and the Caribbean and Central America seem to be the subregions that best take advantage of the time dimension of their proximity to the U.S. market. They have averages that are above East Asia's (whose exports are dominated by fast-to-be-obsolete high-tech products) and well above the average of all other exporters (excluding LAC, Canada and East Asia). On the other end of the spectrum are the Andean countries and, somewhat surprisingly, Mexico.

These figures, though, can be driven by other factors that affect patterns of trade and, to have a sense of the importance of their influence, we use a simple econometric model to test how the revealed comparative advantage of LAC's exports to the United States reacts to product-specific time costs (measured as above), once you net out the influence of the weight-to-value ratios and factor intensity of the products.

By revealed comparative advantage, we mean an indicator that divides the share of a product in the country's exports to the United States by the share of this product in total U.S. imports. With that we want to make sure that if we see that a product has a significant share of the country's exports to the United States, this is not because the U.S. economy spends more on this product. The weight-to-value ratios are included to distinguish the "heavy" from the "time factor" and factor intensity—that is, how intensively each product uses factors such as capital, labor and land—is there to filter out the traditional sources of comparative advantage. In the absence of better information, a number of categorical variables are used as a proxy for the variation of factor intensity across products. The categorical variables are based on Lall's (2000) product classification, which divides goods into five categories: primary goods and resource-based, low-, medium- and high-tech manufactures. We use U.S. merchandise import data from 2000–2006.[13]

---

[12] Formally, the average time cost per day of LAC's subregional exports is calculated as:

$$\tau_j = \sum_k s_i^k * \tau^k$$

where τ_j is the average time cost per day of the exports of country j to the United States, S_j^k is the share of product k in country j exports to the United States. The figures for regions and subregions are simple averages of the countries included.

[13] The model draws on Hummels (2007b). See Appendix 1.B.2 for the model specification and results.

Figure 1.13. The Impact of Time Costs and Weight on LAC's Revealed Comparative Advantages, U.S. Market, 1994–2006

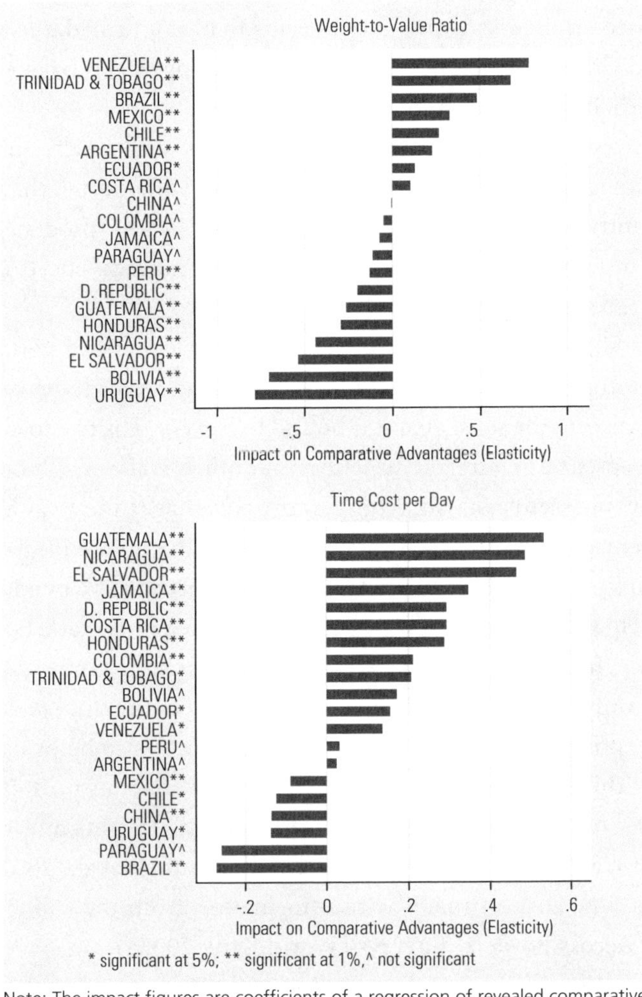

Note: The impact figures are coefficients of a regression of revealed comparative advantages on time costs and weight-to-ratio with controls. See text for details.

Figure 1.13 presents the results and shows how our "variables of interest"—time costs and weight-to-value—impact the countries' revealed comparative advantages in the U.S. market. We have also included the results for China to give us some out-of-the-region perspective. It is clear that the ranking shown in Figure 1.12 changes somewhat, but Central America and the Caribbean remain among those who rely the most on time-sensitive products to penetrate in the U.S. market, followed by the Andean countries, whose exports come out more time sensitive than in the previous ranking. At the bottom of the spectrum lies Mexico, whose low reliance on time-sensitive goods seems to be confirmed, the Southern Cone and China, for whom time sensitiveness appears to have a negative effect on their revealed comparative advantages.

The results on weight-to-value do not show such a clear subregional pattern, but roughly reverse the time-cost ranking, with most of the Southern Cone countries and Mexico relying the most on "heavy" products and the majority of Central American countries showing negative effects of weight on their trade positions.

Overall, whether driven by "heavy" or time-sensitive goods, LAC's revealed comparative advantage in the U.S. market seems to be very transport intensive, in the sense that it is bound to be very sensitive to changes in transport costs, be that freight, time costs or both. It is also worth noting that China does not seem to have its comparative advantage in any way associated with either time-sensitive or "heavy" goods, shoring up the idea, discussed earlier, that the transport intensity of LAC's exports can be one important asset to help the region to prevail in the U.S. and regional markets.

Time, freight and tariffs—Hummels and Schaur's time cost indicator is not only useful to rank countries according to the time sensitiveness of their exports (or imports, for that matter), but it also helps us to illustrate how this somewhat hidden time dimension of transport costs fares against the other more visible trade costs such as freights and tariffs. In Figure 1.14, we follow the approach used by Hummels et al. (2007), which combines time cost estimates with information from the *Doing Business* "Trading Across Borders" Surveys (World Bank 2007a).

What this exercise does is to multiply the number of days that exporters take to get their goods through local transportation, customs and ports by the average time cost per day of the countries' exports. The result is the amount of money exporters spend just to move their goods beyond borders, shown as a percentage of the value of exports. It does not include the time costs arising from delays in transit time between borders, which would give a more realistic picture of how time matters, but it is a good step in this direction.

Figure 1.14. Time and Trade Costs to Export to the U.S., Selected LAC and East Asian Countries, 2006

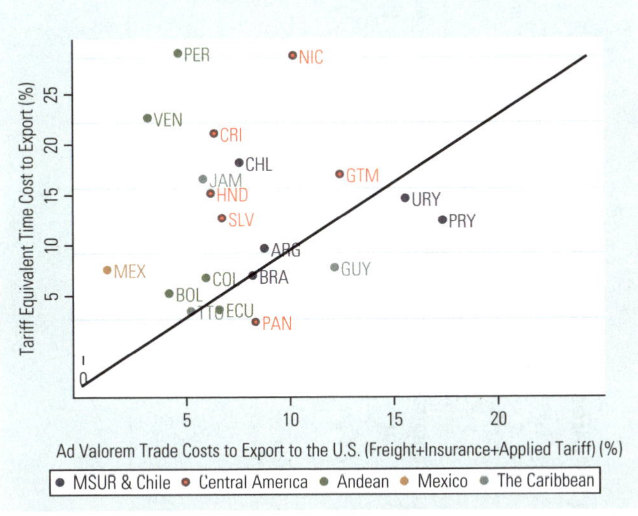

Source: Hummels and Schaur (2007) and *Doing Business* (World Bank 2007a).

As can be seen, for the overall majority of countries in the region the average time costs to get goods across the border are higher than the more traditional trade costs to export to the United States (countries above the diagonal) and in some cases considerably so. These figures are driven not only by relatively high time sensitiveness of some of the LAC countries' exports to the United States, but also by the fact that the region on average fares poorly in terms of the time needed to get goods outside the country. LAC's average number of days to export in 2007 (22.4) was roughly twice the OECD average (9.8) (World Bank 2007a).

The order of magnitude seen in Figure 1.14 is probably not far from the picture for exports to other markets and could not be a better reminder that, when we look at the freight expenditures alone, we have only a partial view of the challenges that lie ahead for the region. Overall, it greatly reinforces the perception that by focusing mainly on bringing tariffs down, LAC's trade policy has been leaving other very important trade costs behind. In the following chapters of this report, we endeavor to drive this point home by looking in more detail at the determinants and impact on trade of the region's transport costs.

Appendix 1.A
Data Tables

Table 1.A.1. Ad Valorem Freight and Real Tariffs for Intra- and Extraregional Imports

Selected LAC Countries. 2005 (%)

	Weighted Average				Simple Average			
Country	Extraregional Freight	Extraregional Tariff	Intraregional Freight	Intraregional Tariff	Extraregional Freight	Extraregional Tariff	Intraregional Freight	Intraregional Tariff
Argentina	4.8	7.3	4.2	0.4	7.8	11.9	6.5	3.5
Brazil	5.1	5.3	6.3	0.6	11.6	11.1	8.7	4.0
Chile	7.1	4.5	7.4	1.9	11.1	4.0	9.5	1.6
Colombia	6.5	5.3	6.3	5.3	10.3	40.9	11.6	58.6
Peru	8.1	9.1	8.3	6.6	11.2	10.3	11.3	8.5
Paraguay	20.1	13.2	5.9	8.0	33.5	17.3	6.7	9.1
Uruguay	6.0	4.2	4.6	0.3	8.9	10.7	5.5	1.5

Note: Freight is the ratio of freight expenditures to imports. Real tariff is the ratio of tariff revenue to imports. Tariff data for Paraguay and Colombia is for 2000 and 2003, respectively. The weighted average was calculated using imports as weight.

Source: Author's calculations based on ALADI data.

Table 1.A.2. Ad Valorem Freight and Real Tariffs for Intraregional Exports and Exports to the U.S.

Selected LAC Countries. 2005 (%)

	Weighted Average				Simple Average			
Country	Freight to the U.S.	U.S. Tariff	Intraregional Freight	Intraregional Tariff	Freight to the U.S.	U.S. Tariff	Intraregional Freight	Intraregional Tariff
Argentina	8.1	1.1	7.2	1.8	14.3	3.7	7.2	1.7
Bolivia	4.9	0.1	13.7	0.1	12.2	2.0	11.7	2.5
Brazil	7.3	1.6	4.7	0.8	12.3	3.4	7.7	2.0
Chile	11.6	0.3	5.1	1.2	13.0	1.3	9.1	4.0
Colombia	6.6	0.2	2.6	1.0	9.4	2.0	4.6	1.7
Ecuador	8.0	0.1	4.3	4.4	15.7	2.3	7.4	1.7
Mexico	1.3	0.1	3.3	2.5	4.2	0.6	8.1	6.5
Peru	5.3	0.1	2.6	0.3	11.8	1.9	6.4	2.7
Paraguay	20.9	3.3	5.2	0.5	13.6	4.7	8.8	1.7
Uruguay	7.2	12.7	4.0	1.4	13.8	4.8	6.4	2.3
Venezuela	3.9	0.1	6.6	2.0	11.2	1.9	10.8	4.5

Note: This table uses import data from the relevant export markets. Freight is the ratio of freight expenditures to imports. The weighted average was calculated using imports as weight. Real tariff is the ratio of tariff revenue to imports. Real tariff is the ratio of tariff revenue to imports. Intraregional export includes Brazil, Argentina, Chile, Peru and Uruguay.

Source: Author's calculations based on ALADI data.

Appendix 1.B
Specification of Empirical Models

1.B.1. Trends in Transport Costs

The model follows Hummels (2007a) and has the following OLS specification:

$$\ln \frac{f_{ijt}^{k}}{v_{ijt}^{k}} = \beta_0 + \beta_1 \ln \frac{WGT_{ijt}^{k}}{v_{ijt}^{k}} + y_t + \alpha_j^k + e_{ijt}^{k}, \tag{1}$$

where

$$\frac{f_{ijt}^{k}}{v_{ijt}^{k}}$$

is the ad valorem freight rate of good *k* from exporter *j* to importer *i*, at time *t*;

$$\frac{WGT_{ijt}^{k}}{V_{ijt}^{k}}$$

is the weight-to-value ratio of the good *k* bought by importer *i*, from exporter *j; y_t* is the vector of year fixed effects; α_j^k is the vector of commodity-exporter fixed effects; β_0 is constant and e_{ijt}^{k} is the error term.

The model is run by country for both world imports (pooling ALADI 6-digit HS data for 1995 and 2000–05 in the case of LAC countries, and pooling U.S. Census Bureau 6-digit HS data for 1995–2005 in the case of the United States) and exports to the United States (pooling U.S. Census Bureau 6-digit HS data for 1994–2006).

The import version of the model includes separate commodity-exporter intercepts α_j^k and year dummies y_t. The former controls for compositional changes (goods and partners) and the (exponentiated) values of the latter are interpreted as the countries' ad valorem freight expenditures over the period after controlling for changes in trade composition. The export-to-the-U.S. version of the model is similar to the import model except for the fact that we include only commodity intercepts instead of partner-commodity intercepts since there is no variation in *i*.

Table 1.B.1. Trends in Import Freight

Pooled OLS 1995–05 Results

	Argentina	Brazil	Chile	Colombia	Peru	Uruguay	U.S.
			Airfreight				
Weight-to-Value Ratio	0.495	0.696	0.447	0.540	0.624	0.299	0.486
	(0.0010)***	(0.0006)***	(0.0018)***	(0.0011)***	(0.0018)***	(0.0029)***	(0.0004)***
Obs.	793,241	2,086,350	379,673	688,673	293,448	158,848	9,900,000
***R*-squared**	0.64	0.75	0.65	0.63	0.76	0.56	0.467
			Ocean				
Weight-to-Value Ratio	0.296	0.665	0.325	0.487	0.612	0.214	0.454
	(0.0009)***	(0.0007)***	(0.0016)***	(0.0011)***	(0.0015)***	(0.0023)***	(0.0006)***
Obs.	1024146	2,319,648	560,359	907,088	457,135	224,117	8,800,000
***R*-squared**	0.61	0.73	0.63	0.65	0.76	0.53	0.3769

Note: The coefficients of the year dummies available upon request.
Robust standard errors in parentheses.* significant at 10%; ** significant at 5%; *** significant at 1%.

Source: ALADI and U.S. Census Bureau.

We run the models with and without outliers (defined as those observations for which

$$\frac{f_{ijt}^k}{v_{ijt}^k} \text{ and } \frac{WGT_{ijt}^k}{v_{ijt}^k}$$

are below or above the first and 99th percentiles of the whole sample), but since there was no noticeable change we present the results derived from the whole sample.

1.B.2. Time Costs and Comparative Advantage

The model draws on Hummels (2007). We run a regression for each country with the following specification:

$$\ln \frac{X_{US\_jt}^k / X_{US\_jt}}{X_{US\_Wt}^k / X_{US\_wt}} = \beta_0 + \beta_1 \ln \tau^k + \beta_2 \ln \frac{W_{us\_j}^k}{v_{us\_j}^k} + a_t + a_k + e_{ijt}^k \qquad (2)$$

where,

$X_{US\_jt}^k / X_{US\_jt}$ is country *j*'s exports of good *k* to the United States as a share of total exports of country *j* to the United States at time *t*; $X_{US\_Worldt}^k / X_{US\_Worldt}$ is world exports of good *k* to the United States as a share of total world exports to the United States at time *t*; τ^k is the tariff equivalent time cost per day of good *k*;

$$\frac{W_{us\_j}^k}{v_{us\_j}^k}$$

is the weight-to-value ratio of good *k*; a_t are the year fixed effects; a^k are the goods category fixed effects and e_{ijt}^k is the error term. The results are shown in Table 1.A.1.

Table 1.B.2. Trends in Export Freight

Pooled OLS 1993–06 Results

	Central America	Mercosur & Chile	Andean	Caribbean	Mexico	China	ROW
			Airfreight				
Weight-to-Value Ratio	0.4925	0.5027	0.4765	0.4093	0.4695	0.6277	0.4781
	(0.0048)***	(0.0029)***	(0.0040)***	(0.0048)***	(0.0027)***	(0.0017)***	(0.0004)***
Obs.	104,769	185,159	127,851	79,636	201,814	680,000	8,600,000
***R*-squared**	0.4727	0.515	0.4947	0.5406	0.4573	0.4178	0.4592
			Ocean				
Weight-to-Value Ratio	0.4659	0.544	0.4245	0.4091	0.4063	0.469	0.4976
	(0.0057)***	(0.0037)***	(0.0082)***	(0.0076)***	(0.0112)***	(0.0016)***	(0.0007)***
Obs.	121,538	290,553	112,357	73,515	29,135	1,200,000	7,500,000
***R*-squared**	0.5105	0.4827	0.5451	0.5197	0.4358	0.3105	0.3435

Note: The coefficients of the year dummies available upon request.

Robust standard errors in parentheses.* significant at 10%; ** significant at 5%; *** significant at 1%.

Source: ALADI and U.S. Census Bureau.

Table 1.B.3. Pooled OLS Regression of Revealed Comparative Advantage on Time Costs and Weight-to-Value. 2000–2006

Country	Time Cost per Day	Weight-to-Value Ratio	Obs	R^2
Mexico	−0.09	0.33	6967	0.0338
	(3.85)**	(15.06)**		
Guatemala	0.533	−0.265	2959	0.0864
	(8.91)**	(4.32)**		
El Salvador	0.466	−0.54	2245	0.1043
	(7.21)**	(8.07)**		
Honduras	0.288	−0.295	1801	0.0788
	(3.43)**	(3.95)**		
Nicaragua	0.487	−0.44	1070	0.1494
	(4.58)**	(4.41)**		
Costa Rica	0.293	0.105	2458	0.0872
	(4.79)**	−1.89		
Jamaica	0.347	−0.073	941	0.1658
	(3.00)**	−0.64		
Dominican Republic	0.294	−0.201	3369	0.0429
	(5.82)**	(3.72)**		
Trinidad & Tobago	0.207	0.683	914	0.3511
	(2.02)*	(7.07)**		
Colombia	0.212	−0.049	4513	0.0198
	(5.60)**	−1.21		
Venezuela	0.137	0.784	2197	0.4019
	(2.46)*	(14.37)**		
Ecuador	0.156	0.13	2394	0.2633
	(2.45)*	(2.44)*		
Peru	0.031	−0.13	3465	0.0769
	−0.6	(2.99)**		
Bolivia	0.171	−0.707	1204	0.184
	−1.86	(8.26)**		
Chile	−0.125	0.268	2797	0.3237
	(2.51)*	(5.39)**		
Brazil	−0.272	0.485	6967	0.1282
	(8.45)**	(17.11)**		
Paraguay	−0.259	−0.112	481	0.3674
	−1.64	−0.84		
Uruguay	−0.139	−0.787	1475	0.1672
	(2.09)*	(9.11)**		
Argentina	0.025	0.232	4212	0.2338
	−0.66	(5.67)**		
China	−0.137	−0.005	11534	0.1231
	(7.18)**	−0.24		

Note: Absolute value of *t* statistics in parenthesis. *significant at 5 %; ** significant at 10%.

References

Batista da Silva, Eliezer. 1996. *Infrastructure for Sustainable Development and Integration in South America.* Monterrey, Mexico: Business Council for Sustainable Development — Latin America (BSCD) and Corporación Andina de Fomento (CAF).

Evans, L. Carolyn, and James Harrigan. 2005. Distance, Time, and Specialization: Lean Retailing in General Equilibrium. *American Economic Review 95: 292–313.*

Harrigan, James. 2005. *Airplanes and Comparative Advantage.* Working Paper 11688. Cambridge, MA: National Bureau of Economic Research.

Hummels, David. 2001. Toward a Geography of Trade Costs. Unpublished manuscript. West Lafayette, IN: Purdue University.

Hummels, David. 2007a. Transportation Costs and International Trade in the Second Era of Globalization. *Journal of Economic Perspectives.* 21: 131–154.

Hummels, David. 2007b. Sources of Export Growth in Latin America. Paper prepared for IDB report. Washington, D.C.: Inter-American Development Bank.

Hummels, David, Peter Minor, Matthew Reisman, and Erin Endean. 2007. Calculating Tariff Equivalents for Time in Trade. Prepared for USAID Bureau of Economic Growth, Agriculture and Trade under Contract No. GS-10F-0619N, Task Order No. EEM-M-00-06-00028-00. Arlington, VA: Nathan Associates Inc.

Hummels, David, and Georg Schaur. 2007. *Time as a Trade Barrier.* Working Paper. West Lafayette, IN: Purdue University (NBER Working Paper, forthcoming).

IDB (Inter-American Development Bank). 2002. *Beyond Borders: The New Regionalism in Latin America.* Economic and Social Progress in Latin America 2002 Report. Washington, D.C.: IDB.

Lall, S. 2000. The Technological Structure and Performance of Developing Country Manufactured Exports, 1985–98. *Oxford Development Studies* 28(3): 337–369.

World Bank. 2004. *Reforming Infrastructure: Privatization, Regulation and Competition.* Washington, D.C.: Oxford University Press for the World Bank.

World Bank. 2007a. *Doing Business 2008.* Washington, D.C.: World Bank.

World Bank. 2007b. *Connecting to Compete: Trade Logistics in the Global Economy 2007.* Washington, D.C.: World Bank.

World Economic Forum. 2007. *Global Competitiveness Report 2007–2008.* Geneva: World Economic Forum.

Determinants of Transport Costs and Implications for LAC

We have seen so far that transport costs are the dominant form of trade costs for LAC, the more so when time costs are taken into account. We have also seen that, in general, the region spends proportionally more on transport to trade its goods than the United States, Europe and Asia. In this chapter, we try to shed some light on what is behind those expenses by analyzing the determinants of transport costs in LAC and elsewhere and what governments can do to reduce them.

In spite of the relevance of the topic, there are not many studies that investigate the determinants of transport costs. Moreover, the few studies available tend to emphasize only one aspect of transport costs. For example, Fink, Mattoo and Neagu (2002) explore the determinants of maritime transport costs focusing on the effect of noncompetitive public and private policies. Clark, Dollar and Micco (2005), Blonigen and Wilson (2006) and Wilmsmeier, Hoffman and Sanchez (2006) stress the effect of port efficiency in ocean shipping. Hummels, Lugovskyy and Skiba (forthcoming) investigate price discrimination in the maritime shipping industry and the role it plays in determining transport costs. Studies on non-maritime transport modes are even scarcer. One example, however, is Micco and Serebrisky (2006) in which the authors estimate the effect of open skies agreements on air transport costs.

In this chapter we analyze the impact of several different factors on both ocean and airfreight.[14] We explore the role that different determinants of transport costs have in explaining differences in shipping costs

[14] We exclude the ground transportation mode because of lack of reliable data on distance. There is practically no information regarding the routes taken by a particular shipment and very often even the district of origin is unknown. This generates very imprecise estimates of distance that may bias the results in a significant way.

between LAC and other regions. This approach not only allows us to show what factors actually affect transport costs, but also explore what types of policies are most likely to generate the largest impacts.

We begin with a general description of the factors that lie behind transport costs, followed by an exercise in which we decompose the difference between LAC's export and import freight rates and those of a typical developed country into its various determinants. For data constraints, we use different benchmarks for the export (Netherlands and the EU) and import (U.S.) rate decompositions. We then summarize the main results and highlight the main policy implications for the region.

Factors behind Transport Costs

As explained in Chapter 1, when analyzing transport costs, the first and most studied determinant is geography, particularly distance. Freight charges are expected to increase the greater the distance traveled between the two markets. A second obvious determinant of transport costs is the transportability of the good. Holding value constant, heavier goods normally pay higher ad valorem shipping prices.

The volume of imports is also a factor that affects transport costs. The transport industry is generally associated with scale economies, that is, the cost of transporting a product decreases with the number of units shipped. Most of these economies of scale are at the vessel level, but there can also be scale economies at the port level.[15] For example, some ports charge lower fees per container to larger vessels (Clark et al. 2005). Congestion effects, however, are a force that plays in the opposite direction. That is, transport costs may increase with volume in the presence of congestion.[16]

[15] A large vessel can be sailed at a relatively lower cost than a small one, as doubling the carrying capacity does not require doubling the expenditures incurred in sailing the vessel.

[16] A case study on exports of dairy products in Argentina by Sicra (2007) provides an example of these two opposite forces. According to the author, exporting firms can obtain up to 30 percent discount in freight rates from shipping companies by increasing their export volumes. However, the recent surge of import and export flows that has occurred in the port of Buenos Aires has raised the time to handle containers from 2 to 5 hours which has increased the freight costs.

Trade imbalances between markets can also affect shipping prices. When a ship (or a plane) is forced to travel empty in one of the directions, freight rates tend to be higher as the shipper normally pays for forgone capacity on either the inbound or the outbound trip.

Shipping prices also depend on the degree of market power exercised by the shipping companies. The larger the degree of competition on a commercial route, the lower the shipping price to be expected. One proxy of market power is the number of shipping firms operating on a commercial route. Using information from the ComPair dataset, we calculate that the average number of shipping firms operating between the typical Latin American country and the United States is only one-third of the average number of shipping firms operating between Europe and the United States. This could be a sign that competition in ocean shipping is weak in Latin America. Trade routes involving larger countries, however, tend to have higher trade volumes, more ships and more liner companies operating on them. Figure 2.1 shows that there is a positive relationship between the number

Figure 2.1. Number of Shippers between a Given Exporter and the U.S.

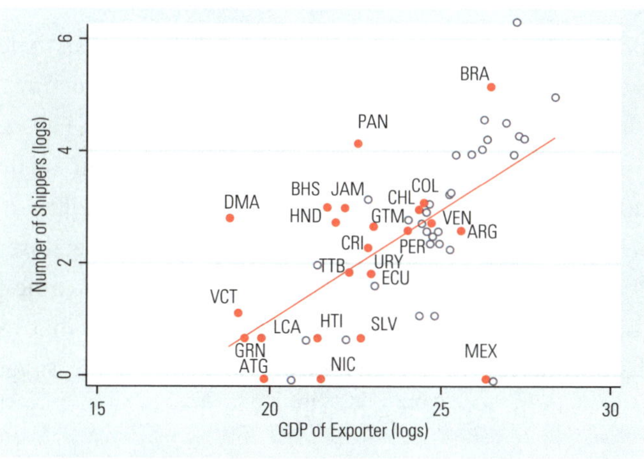

Source: Author's calculation with data from www.compairdataset.com and the World Bank's *World Development Indicators*. The data on GDP is for the average period 2003–2005.

of shippers operating between a given exporter and the United States and the GDP of the exporter (our proxy for size).[17] LAC countries are highlighted in red. Once we control for country size, the picture for Latin America is mixed. While some countries appear below the trend line with low levels of competition for their size, the opposite is true for other countries.

Price discrimination is also a characteristic of the shipping industry (Hummels et al. forthcoming). For instance, the prices that shippers charge in excess of the marginal cost of shipping (or markup) might be larger on goods whose import demand is not very sensitive to price changes. In other words, larger markups are expected on goods with relatively inelastic import demands. Additionally, the optimal markup charged by a shipping firm might increase with product prices (Hummels et al. forthcoming). The intuition behind this argument is that the effect of a given markup on the delivered price of a good is much lower the larger the price of the good. This is the case because the larger the price of the good, the smaller the share of the shipping cost in the delivered price. This implies that anything that raises the price of a good, like a tariff, lowers the percentage impact of a given transportation charge on the delivered price and therefore increases the optimal shipping markup. Given this, we should expect higher shipping charges on goods with larger tariff rates, everything else constant.

A potentially important determinant of transport costs is the level of port efficiency. An improvement in the quality of port infrastructure, for example, may lower transport costs by increasing port efficiency. Figure 2.2 shows a one-to-seven index (with 7 being the best score) of the quality of port infrastructure reported by the World Economic Forum's 2005–2006 *Global Competitiveness Report* (GCR). This index is plotted against GDP per capita.[18] The figure shows that countries with higher income per capita tend to have more efficient ports. The figure also shows that most countries in Latin America (in red dots) lie below the trend line, suggesting that port efficiency in the region is generally lower than expected for the income

---

[17] This relationship was first shown by Hummels et al. (forthcoming).

[18] Data on GDP per capita is in PPP terms, for the average period 2004–2006.

Figure 2.2. Port Efficiency and Income

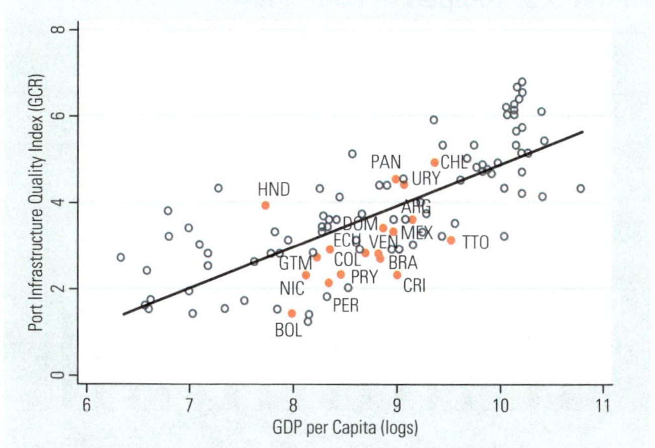

Source: Author's calculation based on data from the *Global Competitiveness Report 2005–2006* (World Economic Forum 2006) and the *Penn World Table* (Heston et al. 2006).

levels observed. Likewise, airport efficiency is also a potentially important determinant of the shipping price in air cargo.

Finally, another factor affecting freight charges, for the particular case of maritime transportation, is the use of containers. Container shipments allow large cost reductions in cargo handling; therefore, lower shipping prices should be expected as the level of containerization increases.

Figure 2.3 shows the percentage of maritime manufactured exports from Latin America to the United States that is shipped in containers.[19] We do not control for differences driven by product composition or container intensity within a given type of product. We will address these issues later in the chapter. Here we only present the raw data to get a preliminary view. In general, the prospects of raising containerization levels in the region are limited as most of the cargo is already shipped in containers. There is, however, some variation across the countries in the region. Some countries present a considerable lag behind the Latin American average and also the average of other regions, suggesting that they are not taking full advantage of the use of containers. As mentioned before, however, these variations might be

---

[19] Data is for the average period 2000–2005.

Figure 2.3. Percentage of Manufactured Exports to the U.S. Shipped in Containers

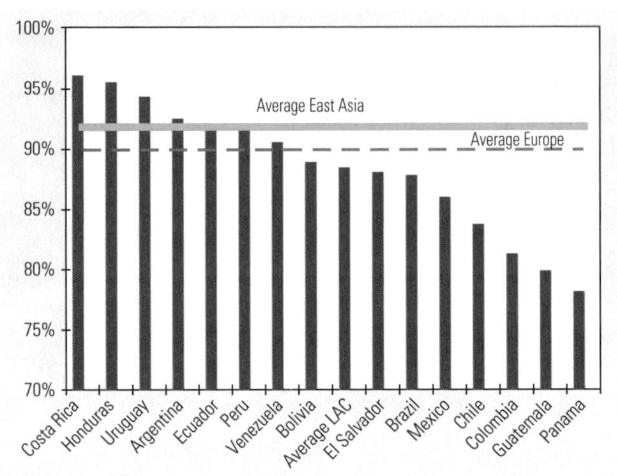

Source: Author's calculation with data from the U.S. Import Waterborne Databanks.

explained by other factors like differences in product composition. We will analyze in detail these issues in our econometric exercise in the next section.

So far we have described what are the likely determinants of transport costs. Next, we measure the impact of these determinants quantitatively.

Explaining Differences in the Costs to Export

In this section we use a dataset that consists of transport charges paid by U.S. imports, taken from the U.S. Waterborne Databanks (U.S. Department of Transportation) (see Data Appendix). Using this data, we compare LAC's export freight rates with those of other exporters to the United States and decompose the difference among its various determinants. The strategy allows us not only to quantify the impact of the determinants of transport costs but also to explore which are the most important factors behind the differences in the shipping costs between LAC and other regions. The analysis starts with ocean freight and proceeds with airfreight.

Table 2.1. Expected Relationships between the Ad Valorem Freight Rates and Their Determinants

Determinants	Expected Sign
Weight-Value	(+)
Distance	(+)
Volume of Imports	(−)
Trade Imbalance	(−)
Containerization	(−)
Number of Shippers	(−)
Elasticity of Import Demand	(−)
Tariff Rate	(+)
Exporter Port Efficiency	(−)
Importer Port Efficiency	(−)

Ocean Freight

Decomposing the difference in transport costs between LAC and other countries into its various determinants requires first estimating a model of transport costs. A complete description of the model is provided in Appendix 2.A. Here we present the basic intuition of the quantitative analysis. Following the discussion in the previous section, we can expect the ad valorem freight rate of a product to increase with the weight of the product, the distance traveled between the two locations and the tariff rate in the destination market. At the same time, we can expect the shipping rate to fall with the volume of imports, the fraction of the imports shipped in containers, the number of shipping firms competing on the particular route, the elasticity of import demand of the product, and the port efficiencies in the exporting and the importing countries and with a change from a favorable to a negative trade imbalance (from the point of view of the exporter) (Table 2.1).

Using very detailed data on ocean freight rates paid by U.S. imports coming from ports in countries around the world, as well as data from several other sources for 2000–2005, we measure quantitatively the impact of these variables on ad valorem freight rates.[20] Detailed results are reported in Table 2.B.1 (in Appendix 2.B).

According to the estimation, goods with higher weight, holding value constant, exhibit higher ad valorem shipping costs, as expected. Freight charges also increase with distance. A doubling in distance, for example, increases transport costs by around 14 percent. The import volume is negatively and significantly correlated with the shipping price, indicating the presence of scale economies in ocean shipping. Directional trade imbalance was also found to be negatively correlated with freight charges. If we move from a favorable imbalance of 25 percent to a negative one of the same amount, transport costs would increase about 8 percent. As expected, there is also a negative (and significant) relationship between the level of containerization and transport costs.

Freight rates also fall with the number of shippers, showing that routes with larger levels of competition tend to have lower markups. As in Hummels et al. (forthcoming), we also find evidence of price discrimination. Shipping prices are higher for goods with lower import demand elasticities, implying that shipping firms are best able to take advantage of their position between producer and consumer to increase markups when consumption decisions are less sensitive to changes in delivered prices. Shipping prices also increase with tariffs, supporting the idea that the optimal markup is a positive function of the tariff level.

We also interact the number of shippers with the import demand elasticity (Table 2.B.1, Appendix 2.B) to explore whether the presence of competition weakens the ability of firms to price discriminate, that is, to charge more on goods with less elastic demands. We find no evidence of this effect, as the coefficient is not significantly different from zero.

We also find that port efficiency, both in the exporting country and in the United States, is a significant determinant of transport costs. Therefore, more efficient ports are associated with lower shipping charges.

Decomposing freight rate differences—We can now use the results from the estimation to decompose the differences in shipping prices

[20] See the Data Appendix of this report for a complete description of all the sources.

Figure 2.4. Decomposing Differences in Ocean Freight Rates between LAC and the Netherlands. Exports to the U.S. (2000–2005)

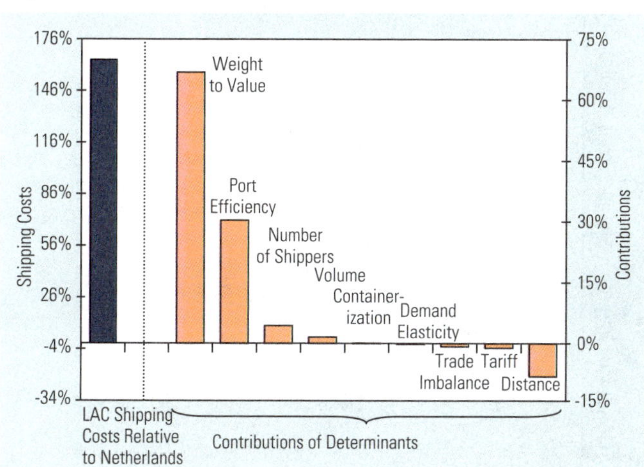

between any two countries (or group of countries) among its various determinants. The decomposition is based on Hummels et al. (forthcoming). In this section the exercise consists of comparing LAC's export freight rates to the United States with those of the Netherlands. We select the Netherlands as the benchmark because the country is often recognized for the quality of its port facilities. The *Global Competitiveness Report 2005–2006* (World Economic Forum 2005), for example, ranks the Netherlands second from a list of 117 countries in terms of port infrastructure quality. The results, however, remain qualitatively the same if we use other benchmarks.

Table 2.2 shows the outcome of the exercise for 11 Latin American countries and for the simple average of the region, while Figure 2.4 depicts the same information graphically for the Latin American average.[21] Although the results vary from country to country, there are well-defined patterns that can be summarized in four points: i) LAC's exports to the United States pay freight rates that are on average 70 percent higher than

[21] These are the countries that have data for all the variables used in the analysis.

Table 2.2. Decomposing Differences in Ocean Freight Rates between LAC and Netherlands Exports to the U.S. (2000–2005)

	LAC Simple Average	Argentina	Brazil	Chile	Colombia	Dominican Republic	Honduras	Mexico	Panama	Peru	Uruguay	Venezuela
Ad Valorem Shipping Costs:												
$\hat{f}_{LAC} / \hat{f}_{NETH}$	168%	196%	217%	230%	135%	127%	108%	142%	167%	153%	162%	157%
Contribution to Differences in Fitted Values:												
Weight-to-Value Ratio	72%	59%	60%	79%	146%	65%	96%	88%	58%	47%	58%	114%
Exporter Port Efficiency	33%	30%	33%	19%	−6%	118%	204%	44%	62%	55%	27%	−4%
Number of Shippers	5%	4%	3%	3%	8%	12%	34%	8%	4%	7%	6%	5%
Volume	2%	1%	1%	3%	3%	3%	7%	2%	3%	2%	3%	3%
Containerization	0%	0%	0%	0%	1%	2%	0%	0%	0%	0%	0%	0%
Demand Elasticity	0%	0%	0%	0%	0%	0%	0%	0%	−1%	0%	−1%	0%
Tariff	−1%	−1%	−1%	−1%	−2%	−2%	2%	−4%	−2%	−1%	1%	−2%
Trade Imbalance	−1%	−1%	0%	1%	4%	−17%	−23%	10%	−13%	−3%	−5%	15%
Distance	−9%	8%	3%	−3%	−54%	−80%	−219%	−49%	−12%	−7%	11%	−30%

Source: Author's calculations based on results from regression (1), Table 2.B.1 (Appendix 2.B). Example of decomposition: to get the contribution of, say, the number of shippers to the difference in shipping prices between Argentina and Netherlands, we calculate the following:

$$\frac{\hat{\beta}_2 (\ln n_{ARG} - \ln n_{NETH})}{\ln \hat{f}_{ARG} - \ln \hat{f}_{NETH}} = \frac{0.027}{0.670} = 0.04$$

where n_{ARG} and n_{NETH} are the sample averages of the number of shippers between Argentina and the U.S. and between the Netherlands and the U.S., respectively. We proceed similarly for each explanatory variable and for each country. For the case of port efficiency we use the simple average of the estimated port fixed effects of the country, or $\hat{\theta}$.

those from the Netherlands; ii) the main factors explaining the differences in the transport costs are the weight-to-value ratios and port efficiency, followed by the levels of competition among shipping companies and, to a lesser degree, the volumes of trade; iii) differences in the level of containerization and in the demand elasticity have very small roles in explaining differences in the shipping costs; and iv) the differences in the tariff rates, trade imbalance and distances tend to play in favor of Latin America in the sense that imports from LAC face, on average, lower tariff in the United States, are associated with more favorable trade imbalances and are shipped from shorter distances than the imports from the Netherlands.

We now elaborate further on these results. First of all, the results from the decomposition show that although there is an obvious effect of distance on costs, this is by no means the only determinant of the shipping price. Using distance as a proxy for transportation costs has been common in the literature, but it only explains a small percentage of the variation in shipping charges. The most important factor behind the difference in the shipping costs between Latin America and the Netherlands comes from weight-to-value ratios. We saw earlier that keeping value constant, heavier goods pay higher freights. As the United States tends to import higher-value goods from the Netherlands than from LAC, the typical basket of imports from the region exhibits a higher weight-to-value ratio than those from the Netherlands and thus higher ad valorem freight expenditures. This part of the difference in shipping prices is therefore entirely due to differences in the composition of the baskets of goods. A discussion on the composition of LAC's export basket goes beyond the scope of this book. What is important from this result is to recognize that the region's export basket involves the transportation of goods that are on average heavier than the export basket from other countries. This is another reason why addressing the issue of transport costs is particularly important for LAC.

One factor with clear tangible policy implications for the countries in the region is port efficiency. According to the decomposition, on average, about 33 percent of the difference in shipping prices between Latin

America and the Netherlands is explained by this factor as the typical port in Latin America is less efficient than the typical port in the Netherlands. This result is in line with other studies that find port efficiency to be an important component of the shipping costs (see Clark et al. 2005 and Blonigen and Wilson 2006).[22]

Similarly to port efficiency, the level of competition among shippers is another factor with potential policy implications for the region. There are fewer shippers servicing the average route between the United States and Latin America than the average route between the United States and the Netherlands. Differences in this factor explain, on average, about 5 percent of the differences in the shipping costs. For countries like Honduras, Dominican Republic, Colombia, Mexico and Peru, however, the contribution of this factor is considerably higher.

Finally, another factor behind the higher shipping costs observed in the region is the lower volume of imports coming from LAC. Although trade volume typically contributes to less than 5 percent of the differences in shipping costs between countries in LAC and the Netherlands, the finding confirms that taking advantage of scale economies is another way by which transport costs can be lowered. Dealing with capacity constraints may be a way to exploit these scale economies. For instance, according to a study prepared for this report (see Chapter 4), freight rates could be reduced in the Paranaíba-Tietê-Paraná waterways of Brazil through investments in harbor dredging that could allow larger ships into the ports, increasing the volume of trade (Batista 2007).

---

[22] Somewhat surprising is the result that Colombia and Venezuela exhibit levels of port efficiency that are, in essence, similar to that of the Netherlands (see Table 2.2). It is important, however, to stress what our measurements of port efficiency capture. Our data only reflects the transport charges incurred in bringing the merchandise from alongside the carrier at the port of export and placing it alongside the carrier at the port of entry. Therefore, our measures of port efficiency only capture factors that affect the shipment costs that are related to navigating the harbor and unloading the goods dockside. There is, however, a whole array of maritime auxiliary services and port services that are not captured by the data. Examples of these are: storage and warehousing, container station and depot, customs clearance, provisioning, fueling and watering, garbage collecting and disposal, shore-based operational services, and emergency repair facilities, among others. All these services might be more efficiently provided in the ports of the Netherlands than in their counterparts in Latin America, but unfortunately, our data does not allow us to capture these effects.

Airfreight

In this subsection we analyze the impact of several different factors on airfreight rates and explore their importance in explaining differences in shipping costs between LAC and other countries. We estimate a model of transport costs using U.S. Bureau of Census data on transport charges paid by U.S. imports. The model is presented in full detail in Appendix 2.A. Here we describe its main characteristics. The factors determining airfreight rates are the same as those behind ocean freight, except for the level of containerization. In fact, the expected relationships between the ad valorem freight rates and their various determinants presented in Table 2.1 apply also for the case of air transportation.

The data used in estimating the model is very similar to that employed in ocean freight. One particular difference, however, is the level of aggregation. In this dataset the origin of the shipment is not differentiated at the airport (port), but at the country level. Therefore, we cannot use the same techniques to measure port efficiencies in the exporting countries (see Appendix 2.A for details). This time we need to use proxies of airport efficiencies at the country level.

Unfortunately, there is not much comparable information about airport efficiency to be used in a cross-country analysis. The efficiency of an airport (or a port), however, is highly correlated to the quality of its infrastructure. Therefore, we use an index of airport infrastructure provided by Micco and Serebrisky (2006) to proxy for airport efficiency. Specifically, the index measures the fraction of the population in a country that has access to an airport with paved runways of at least 2000 meters long and 40 meters wide.[23] To account for the "quality" of airport infrastructure, understood as runway availability per million city inhabitants, the authors interact this share of population with the quantity of runways per million inhabitants.[24]

---

[23] The choice of this runway specification corresponds to the requirements of the standard aircrafts in the air cargo industry (such as the Boeing 757, 727 and DC-8) that have an estimated width of 33 meters and must use a runway at least 1875 meters long when arriving or departing from an airport with an estimated elevation of 2000 feet.

[24] According to the authors, a person who lives in a city that is at most 75 km away from an airport is considered to have access to that airport.

In addition to this proxy of airport availability in the country, we use another variable that seeks to capture the efficiency with which the airports of the country operate. This variable is the volume of airport traffic divided by airport size.[25] Controlling for size, more efficient airports should be able to handle more traffic. However, airports with an excess of traffic might run into congestion problems that could increase the transport costs. Therefore, efficiency arguments would suggest a negative relationship between this variable and the shipping costs while congestion effects would suggest a positive relationship.

The rest of the variables in the model are measured in similar ways as in the ocean freight model (see Appendix 2.A for details). The number of shipping companies, however, is now proxied by the number of airlines operating between the exporting country and the United States. The results of the estimation are shown in Table 2.B.2 in Appendix 2.B. The main findings are described below.

As in ocean freight, rates are found to increase with the weight-to-value ratio, distance, and tariff rate. These relationships are always significant except for the tariff rate, which is significant in two out of the three specifications. The import volume is found to have a positive relationship with the freight rate, but is not statistically significant.

The number of airlines has the expected negative sign, supporting the notion that stronger competition reduces air cargo charges. However, the estimate is not significant at conventional levels. Shipping prices are found to be lower for goods with larger import demand elasticities, indicating that in the air industry shipping firms are also able to increase markups when consumption decisions are less sensitive to changes in delivered prices. The proxy of airport infrastructure availability is found to be negatively correlated with the freight rate, supporting the argument that better airport efficiency is associated with lower shipping costs. Finally, our measure of airport traffic is also found to have a negative association with the ad valorem freight rate, but the relationship is not statistically significant.

---

[25] The variable enters the model at the country level as we take the average of this measure across the major airports of the country (see Appendix 2.A for details).

Decomposing freight rate differences—As in ocean freight, we use the empirical results of the model to decompose the difference in airfreight rates between LAC and a typical developed country. The Netherlands was used as a benchmark in the previous decomposition because the country is recognized worldwide for the quality of its port facilities. Such an obvious comparator is harder to identify for the case of air transportation. Several of the EU-15 countries, however, have airport facilities that are ranked among the world's best (see the World Economic Forum's *Global Competitiveness Report 2007–2008*). Therefore, we use the EU-15 countries as the benchmark in this case. The results do not change in any significant way with the use of other developed country benchmarks. Table 2.3 presents the results.

The first row of the table shows that air-shipping costs in all LAC countries are higher than in Europe. Leaving the weight-to-value ratio aside, the higher shipping costs of the typical LAC country (the average of the sample) is mainly due to differences in airport efficiency. Differences in airport efficiency explain almost half of the differences in the shipping charges between the typical Latin American country and the typical EU-15 country.

Differences in the tariff rate tend to play in favor of LAC, indicating that LAC's exports, on average, face slightly lower tariffs rates in the United States than those of the EU-15. The contribution of the tariff rate, however, is almost insignificant, indicating that the differences in this variable are very small. This is not the case, however, for a country like Mexico that clearly enjoys better market access to the United States than the European countries because of the North American Free Trade Agreement (NAFTA).

Finally, the variable distance tends to play in favor of the Caribbean and Central American countries and against the countries in the Southern Cone. On average, however, the contribution of this variable in explaining differences in the freight rate is relatively small.

Overall, we have found that LAC's exporters pay on average higher ad valorem freight rates than their counterparts in the developed world, both in ocean and air transportation. Although the main reasons differ by country, in general, these higher transport costs are explained mostly by

Table 2.3. Decomposing Differences in Airfreight Rates between LAC and the EU-15 Exports to the U.S. (2000–2005)

	LAC Simple Average	Argentina	Bolivia	Brazil	Chile	Colombia	Ecuador	Guatemala	Guyana	Haiti	Honduras	Mexico	Nicaragua	Paraguay	Peru	Uruguay	Venezuela
Ad Valorem Shipping Cost:																	
$\hat{f}_{LAC} / \hat{f}_{EU\text{-}15}$	127%	137%	110%	170%	142%	127%	129%	121%	131%	126%	112%	106%	128%	142%	122%	104%	112%
Contribution to Differences in Fitted Values:																	
Weight-to-Value Ratio	70%	50%	−44%	50%	57%	69%	67%	111%	96%	92%	125%	125%	114%	66%	45%	−163%	130%
Airport Efficiency	45%	38%	138%	49%	36%	64%	55%	44%	32%	75%	78%	185%	27%	23%	65%	121%	56%
Demand Elasticity	0%	0%	0%	0%	−1%	0%	0%	0%	0%	−1%	1%	1%	−1%	1%	−1%	−2%	1%
Tariff	−1%	0%	3%	−1%	−2%	−2%	0%	2%	−3%	−4%	−4%	−35%	0%	4%	0%	39%	−2%
Distance	−14%	12%	3%	1%	9%	−31%	−22%	−56%	−25%	−62%	−100%	−176%	−41%	6%	−9%	105%	−84%

Source: Author's calculations based on results from regression (3) in Table 2.B.2 (Appendix 2.B). See Table 2.2 for an explanation of this type of decomposition.

differences in the composition of exports, in the levels of port efficiency, and to a lower degree, by the level of competition among shipping firms and the volumes of trade (ocean freight).

Explaining Differences in the Costs to Import

In the previous section we compared the transport costs of LAC's exports to the United States with those of European countries. In this section we focus on transport costs to import, comparing the freight rates of LAC and the United States. Import freights may tell a different story since we are looking at a considerably different set of goods, modes and partners. The analysis is similar to the previous section in the sense that we decompose the differences into various components. The factors explaining transport costs of imports are essentially the same as in the previous section. The purpose of this section is to shed more light, using additional datasets, on what factors are behind the larger transport costs that are observed in Latin America relative to other countries.

We combine the data on ocean freight rates paid by U.S. imports used above with a similar dataset for Brazil, Chile, Ecuador, Peru and Uruguay put together by ALADI.[26] We look at ocean freight first.

Ocean Freight

In this section we employ a model that is similar to the one used for the analysis of the ocean freights to export. In this dataset, however, the observations are for 2005 only and are disaggregated at the country level for the origin of the shipment and at the port level for its destination. Therefore, the data consists of country-to-port pairs. The specific model that is estimated is presented in detail in Appendix 2.A and the results of the estimation are reported in Table 2.B.3 of Appendix 2.B. The main empirical findings can be summarized as follows.

---

[26] Although the ALADI dataset includes 12 countries from Latin America, only Brazil, Chile, Ecuador, Peru and Uruguay have data for all the variables used in the analysis. See the Data Appendix.

Table 2.4. Decomposing Differences in Ocean Freight Rates between LAC and the U.S. Imports (2005)

	LAC Simple Average	Brazil	Chile	Ecuador	Peru	Uruguay
Ad Valorem Shipping Costs:						
$\hat{f}_{LAC} / \hat{f}_{US}$	176%	188%	163%	159%	220%	133%
Contribution to Differences in Fitted Values:						
Weight-to-Value Ratio	39%	48%	41%	46%	44%	−27%
Port Efficiency	36%	16%	46%	55%	35%	53%
Tariff	16%	18%	−2%	23%	14%	39%
Number of Shippers	6%	6%	9%	9%	3%	13%
Demand Elasticity	2%	4%	2%	1%	0%	5%
Distance	2%	8%	3%	−34%	3%	17%

Source: Author's calculations based on results from regression in Table 2.B.3 (Appendix 2.B). See Table 2.2 for an explanation of this type of decomposition.

Consistent with the previous results, ad valorem freight rates are found to increase with the weight-to-value ratio, distance, and the tariff rate. The relationship between freight charges and the import volume is negative, but not statistically significant. Once again, we find evidence that ocean routes with stronger competition (larger number of shippers) tend to have lower markups. Shipping prices are also found to be lower for goods with larger import demand elasticities, as expected. The relationship between port efficiency of the exporter (proxy at the country level) and the freight rate is negative, but not statistically significant in this regression. On the other hand, we found evidence that the port efficiencies of the importing countries are significant determinants of the transport costs. The higher the port efficiency of the importer the lower the shipping costs.

Table 2.4 decomposes the difference in shipping costs between the United States and LAC's imports. The first row indicates that Latin American importers face ocean-shipping costs that are on average 76 percent higher than the shipping costs facing U.S. importers. The next two rows show that 39 percent of these differences arise from differences in the weight-to-value ratio and 36 percent from ports in the typical Latin American country (average of the sample) being less efficient than ports in the United States.

Figure 2.5. Percentage Reductions in Transport Costs from a Change in Port Efficiency, Tariff Rates and Number of Shippers to U.S. Levels, Base Year 2005

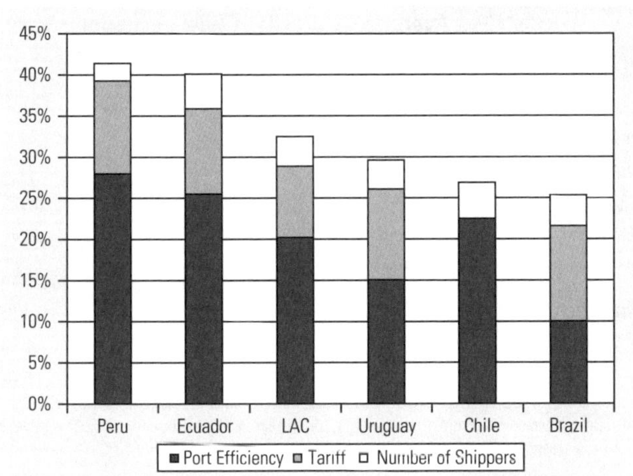

Source: Author's calculations.

A new and interesting insight comes from the results on tariff rates. They account for approximately 16 percent of the difference in the shipping prices between LAC and U.S. imports. This is because LAC countries impose, on average, higher tariffs on their imports than the United States. As the tariff rates are larger, the shipping costs are larger too. Hummels et al. (forthcoming) find a similar result with tariff rates explaining also almost half of the differences in the shipping prices between the two economies. As argued by the authors, these findings suggest that lowering tariffs in Latin America would yield a double impact on trade flows: a direct impact by lowering the tax on imports and an indirect impact by inducing lower shipping prices. Finally, the smaller number of shippers servicing LAC routes explains around 6 percent of the differences in the shipping costs.

Using the results from the regression, Figure 2.5 presents simulations of how much transport costs would be reduced if countries in the region would have the same levels of own port efficiency, tariff rates and shipping competition as in the United States. For the typical Latin American country, the transport costs would be reduced by around 20 percent if port efficiency were improved to the U.S. level. Lowering the tariff rates and increasing competition to the U.S. levels would also reduce transport costs further by 9 and

Table 2.5. Decomposing Differences in Airfreight Rates between LAC and the U.S., Imports (2005)

	LAC Simple Average	Brazil	Chile	Ecuador	Peru	Uruguay
Ad Valorem Shipping Costs:						
$\hat{f}_{LAC} / \hat{f}_{US}$	278%	284%	388%	240%	311%	156%
Contribution to Differences in Fitted Values:						
Weight-to-Value Ratio	48%	20%	56%	65%	44%	42%
Port Efficiency	40%	65%	40%	27%	35%	46%
Tariff	17%	18%	4%	23%	25%	30%
Foreign Infrastructure	0%	−1%	1%	1%	1%	1%
Demand Elasticity	0%	0%	0%	0%	0%	0%
Distance	−6%	−1%	−1%	−16%	−6%	−20%

Source: Author's calculations based on results from the regression in Table 2.B.4 (Appendix 2.B). See Table 2.2 for an explanation of this type of decomposition.

4 percent, respectively. The exercise serves to illustrate that the potential reductions in transport costs arising through these channels could be important, particularly for some countries.

Air Transport Costs

Finally, we combine the data on air transport charges paid by U.S. imports with a similar dataset for LAC put together by ALADI. The set of countries and the model specifications are the same as for ocean freight (see Appendix 2.A for details). Table 2.B.4 in Appendix 2.B presents the results of the estimation. The empirical findings tend to be in line with the previous results for airfreight, with variables such as distance, weight to value, volume, tariffs and infrastructure quality presenting the expected and statistically significant impacts.

Table 2.5 presents the decomposition exercise. The first row shows that the difference in air shipping costs between LAC and U.S. imports is even larger than that for ocean freight shown in Table 2.4. LAC airfreight rates are more than twice those of the United States. The other rows show the contributions of each factor. Leaving the contribution of the weight-to-value ratio aside, a large part of the difference in the shipping prices is once again explained by airport efficiency. LAC airports tend to be less efficient than those of the United States and this explains around 40 percent of the difference in shipping charges. The role of import tariffs is also important. Higher tariffs in LAC explain on average about 17 percent of the differences in the shipping costs. Except for distance, which tends to play in favor of Latin American countries, the contributions of the other variables are insignificant.

Summing Up

The evidence reviewed in this chapter strongly suggests that shipping costs for both LAC imports and exports are considerably and consistently higher than those seen in developed economies such as Europe and the United States. A substantial part of this difference—especially in the case of exports—appears to be explained by LAC trade being "heavier" than that of its developed counterparts. This reinforces the point made earlier in Chapter 1 that heavier trade implies that transport costs tend to be relatively more important to the region's economy than to those of the United States and Europe.

The evidence also suggests that once we net out the influence of trade composition, factors that are related to the efficiency of the countries' infrastructure explain the bulk of the difference between LAC and its developed partners. Distance generally plays only a minor role. This is good and bad news for LAC policy makers. The good news is that reducing transport costs is within reach of policy makers as long as they adopt the right policies and make the necessary investments to boost the efficiency of the transport infrastructure. The bad news is that inefficient logistic chains can quickly and easily erode the region's proximity advantage to large markets such as the United States.

Good or bad, the empirical analysis suggests that there is clearly a need for government action and provides a number of valuable insights on what the priorities should be. The first has to do with port and airport efficiency, which generally explains about 40 percent of the differences in shipping costs between LAC and the United States and Europe. The estimations suggest, for example, that improving port efficiency to the level of

U.S. ports could reduce ad valorem freight rates of Latin American imports by an average of 20 percent.

Many factors affect port and airport efficiency. In the case of ports, for example, their efficiency is related not only to the quality of their facilities, but also to the various other support activities, such as pilotage, towing and tug assistance, or cargo handling. Port efficiency also depends on aspects such as the clarity of port procedures, the accuracy of the information systems or the quality of the vessel traffic system used in the port. There are also legal restrictions, such as requiring special licenses to operate stevedoring services, that can influence the performance of a port. All these factors affect the costs associated with port activities and thus its efficiency. Similarly, the efficiency of an airport depends on the quality of its infrastructure, the related cargo handling activities as well as the existing legal restrictions.

Another factor with potential policy implications for LAC countries is the degree of competition among shipping companies. The analysis indicates that in general fostering competition can lower the shipping costs in LAC. Our results were statistically significant for ocean, but not for airfreight. These mixed results, however, seem to reflect more than anything the difficulty in measuring with accuracy the actual degree of competition in air routes. Particularly, the dataset on air carriers—our proxy for the level of competition in the airline industry—presents some shortcomings. For one, the smaller carriers operating between trade routes are not always included. For another, due to limitations of the freight database, the number of shippers could not be measured between airport pairs, as in ocean freight, but between country pairs. This might give a less accurate picture of the actual degree of competition that exists in air trade routes.

Recent events, in Brazil, for instance, speak volumes about the magnitude of the distortions and, therefore, about the potential for gains. ANAC—Brazil's regulatory agency for civil aviation—decided in September 2007 to eliminate minimum price restrictions on air ticket prices to South America. According to the agency, because of these restrictions, return flights, for instance, from São Paulo, Brazil's second largest city, to Buenos Aires, Argentina's capital, can cost up to 814 percent more (!) than a return ticket from Buenos Aires to São Paulo. Unlike Brazil, Argentina does not impose minimum prices on tickets for that route.[27]

Looking beyond our empirical results, there are many reasons to believe that poor competition in the airline industry contributes substantially to the high freight rates in the region. For example, as discussed in Chapter 4, the regulatory framework in a country such as Ecuador—by any means an exception in the region—does not promote competition among air carriers, limiting the efficiency with which the air transportation system operates and increasing shipping costs. In general, the regulatory framework of the aviation industry in LAC is very restrictive.[28] Contrary to the trends towards the liberalization that has occurred in other parts of the world, the markets for air services in Latin America still depend on complex bilateral air services agreements that often impose limits to the level of competition that is allowed particularly on main international routes. The regulatory frameworks that currently exist often protect inefficient operators that tend to pass their high costs to the final users.

In ocean freight, there has been more progress in liberalizing the industry in the region. Most of the countries in LAC are already open to international competition although some bilateral agreements still exist (Hoffman 2000). Most of the current restrictions that still affect maritime transport efficiency are limited to cabotage, which is present in many countries around the world. However, some countries such as the United Kingdom have liberalized cabotage completely.

It is worth mentioning that the beneficial impact of competition on transport costs might not be limited to the actual transportation services. In ocean freight, for example, a whole array of auxiliary services and port services can be allocated competitively. Examples of these services are: storage and warehousing, provisioning, fueling and watering, shore-based operational services and emergency repair facilities. Note that in this aspect, competition and port efficiency become interrelated. That is, competition

---

[27] See Globo online http://oglobo.globo.com/pais/mat/2007/09/20/297801549.asp

[28] For a comprehensive review of the air transportation agreements in South America see Ricover and Negre (2004).

has an impact on transport costs because it affects the degree of port efficiency. Indeed, evidence of improvement in port performance and reduction of costs after auxiliary services were competitively commissioned can be found, for example, in Trujillo and Estache (2001) and Foxley and Mardones (2000).[29]

This chapter also shows that increases in tariff rates lead to increases in transportation costs. This is our third empirical finding with clear policy implications for LAC. We show, for example, that around 17 percent of the differences in shipping prices between LAC and U.S. imports can be explained by differences in tariff rates as LAC countries impose, on average, higher tariffs on their imports than the United States. This implies that further lowering tariffs in the region, particularly in the large countries of the Southern Cone, has the potential to yield a double impact on trade flows: a direct impact by lowering the tax on imports and an indirect impact by inducing lower shipping prices.

The analysis also provides some evidence, although not always robust, that the lack of scale and the level of containerization play a limited role in the high shipping costs seen in the region. On scale, the case studies of soy in Brazil and cut flowers in Ecuador discussed in Chapter 4 provide some vivid examples of how low volumes can raise shipping costs and hurt exports. Overall, though, this is a problem that reflects the relatively small size of the region's economies and the most policy makers can do is to promote hub-and-spoke transport networks. On containerization, there is also limited scope for government action since a significant part of the region's exports, that is, grains and minerals, cannot be transported by containers and most countries in the region already exhibit large containerization levels of their manufacturing exports.

[29] Note that our analysis does not address this particular aspect of the transportation costs because the data does not capture the price of maritime auxiliary services. More specifically, the data only reflects the transport charges incurred in bringing the merchandise from alongside the carrier at the port of export and placing it alongside the carrier at the port of entry.

Appendix 2.A
Specification of Empirical Models

2.A.1. Ocean Freight Model for Exports

For this model we use data on maritime transport charges paid by U.S. imports from countries around the world during the period 2000–2005. Following Clark et al. (2005), Blonigen and Wilson (2006) and Hummels et al. (forthcoming) we employ a reduced form equation for the cost of transporting goods by ocean. The particular specification to be estimated is the following:

$$\ln\frac{F_{ijkt}}{V_{ijkt}} = \beta_0 + \beta_1 \ln\frac{WGT_{ijkt}}{V_{ijkt}} + \beta_2 \ln DIST_{ij} + \beta_3 \ln q_{ijt} + \beta_4 Timb_{It} \quad (1)$$
$$+ \beta_5 T_{ijkt} + \beta_6 \ln n_{ij} + \beta_7 \ln \lambda_{Ikt} + \beta_8 \ln \sigma_k + \phi_i + \theta_j + \gamma_k + \tau_t + e_{ijkt}$$

where

$$\frac{F_{ijkt}}{V_{ijkt}}$$

is the freight-to-value ratio (or ad valorem freight rate) of product k transported between locations i and j in year t; (i) indexes foreign ports; (j) indexes U.S. ports and (k) indexes products at the 6-digit Harmonized System level.

$$\frac{WGT_{ijkt}}{V_{ijkt}}$$

is the weight-to-value ratio of good k transported between i and j, $DIST_{ij}$ is the distance between locations i and j, q_{ijt} is the total volume of imports (in kilograms) carried by ocean between locations i and j,[30] $Timb_{It}$ is the maritime trade imbalance between country I and the United States and is measured as the difference between maritime exports and imports divided by total maritime trade, T_{ijkt} is the fraction of k goods shipped between locations i and j in containers, n_{ij} is the number of shippers between locations i

[30] It is worth noting that since we use weight as our quantity measure for the volume of imports, we have two separate measures of scale: the numerator in the weight-to-value ratio and the volume of imports. Therefore, the total derivative of freight costs with respect to weight is equal to β_1 divided by value plus β_3.

and j, λ_{Ikt} is the effective ad valorem tariff that country I faces in the United States for good k, σ_k is the elasticity of import demand of good k, ϕ_i is a set of fixed effects parameters that estimate the separate impact of each foreign (or exporter) port, θ_j are the equivalent port fixed effects for the United States (these are our measures of port efficiency in this specification), γ_k are product fixed effects (at the 2-digit HS level) that control for unobserved product characteristics beyond the weight-to-value ratio and the import demand elasticity, τ_t is a set of year effects and e_{ijkt} is the error term.

The data on freight, trade values, weight and containerization levels come from the U.S. Waterborne Databanks (U.S. Department of Transportation). Import duties are calculated with data from the U.S. Census Imports of Merchandise. Distance from port to port is taken from Shipanalysis. We use estimates of σ_k at 6-digit HS taken from Broda and Weinstein (2006). The number of shippers from port to port is calculated using information from www.ComPair.com. The data appendix of this report presents a detailed description of all these datasets. The results of this estimation are presented in Table 2.B.1 in Appendix 2.B.

The use of port dummies in equation (1) could affect the estimation of the variables that have only variation across i and j, like the number of shippers. For this reason, we also run two alternative specifications to this model. The first specification uses a two-step procedure. In the first step we follow Blonigen and Wilson (2006) and run equation (1) without the number of shippers, the tariff rate and the elasticity of import demand. From this regression we obtain the estimated values of the port fixed effects. In the second step we run equation (1) again but without the port fixed effects and use the estimated values of the port fixed effects obtained from the first step regression. This procedure eliminates entirely the use of port dummies in the final specification.

The second alternative model consists of controlling for the level of port efficiency not at the port level as in equation (1) but at the country level using country fixed effects. Therefore, in this model we drop all the port fixed effects of the exporting countries and use country fixed effects instead. Once again, this minimizes the use of port dummies. The results from both specifications are very similar to the results presented in Table 2.B.1 (available upon request).

2.A.2. Airfreight Model for Exports

For this model we employ data on transport charges paid by U.S. imports from countries around the world. The sample period is 2000–2005. One difference with the previous model is the level of aggregation of the data. In this case, the origin of the shipment is not differentiated at the port (airport) level but at the country level. This requires a slight change in the model. The exact specification to be estimated is the following:

$$\ln\frac{F_{ikt}}{V_{ikt}} = \beta_0 + \beta_1 \ln\frac{WGT_{ikt}}{V_{ikt}} + \beta_2 \ln DIST_i + \beta_3 \ln q_{it} + \beta_4 \ln n_i + \beta_5 \ln\lambda_{ikt} + \beta_6 \ln\sigma_k + \beta_7 \ln INF_i + \gamma_k + \tau_t + e_{ikt} \quad (2)$$

where

$$\frac{F_{ikt}}{V_{ikt}}$$

is the ad valorem freight rate for product k imported from country i to the United States,

$$\frac{WGT_{ikt}}{V_{ikt}}$$

is the weight-to-value ratio of product k imported from country i, $DIST_i$ is the distance between country i and the United States, q_{it} is the total volume of imports (in kilograms) carried by air from country i, n_i is the number of airlines with services between country i and the United States, λ_{ikt} is the effective ad valorem tariff that country i faces in the United States for good k, σ_k is the elasticity of import demand of good k, INF_i is a measure of airport infrastructure in country i to proxy for airport efficiency, γ_k are product fixed-effect parameters, τ_t is the set of year effects and e_{ikt} is the error term.[31]

Data on freight, value, weight and import duties come from the U.S. Imports of Merchandise (U.S. Census Bureau). For distance we use the great-circle distance between capitals. The number of airlines is taken from ICAO (the Data Appendix presents a detailed description of the U.S. Census Imports of Merchandise and the ICAO datasets).

[31] The variable trade imbalance is not included because there is no data on U.S. exports for the air mode.

A measure of airport infrastructure availability is provided by Micco and Serebrisky (2006).[32] We also include a variable that seeks to reflect the efficiency with which airports operate. This variable is the volume of airport traffic divided by airport size. Specifically, we first take the volume of freight in metric tons of each major airport of a country and divide it by the total lengths of its runways (our proxy of airport size). Then we calculate the country's weighted average of this measure where the weights are each of the airport's share in total traffic. The data on airport traffic comes from ICAO. The data on airport runway length is taken from www.airportcitycodes.com. The results of this estimation are presented in Table 2.B.2 in Appendix 2.B.

2.A.3. Ocean Freight Model for Imports

For this model we combine the data on maritime transport charges paid by U.S. imports used in section 2.3 with similar datasets for various Latin American countries put together by ALADI. The countries included in the analysis are Brazil, Chile, Ecuador, Peru and Uruguay, in addition to the United States. The specific model takes the following functional form:

$$\ln\frac{F_{ijkt}}{V_{ijkt}} = \beta_0 + \beta_1 \ln\frac{WGT_{ijkt}}{V_{ijkt}} + \beta_2 \ln DIST_{ij} + \beta_3 \ln q_{ijt} + \beta_4 \ln n_{ij} + \beta_5 \ln\lambda_{ijkt} + \beta_6 \ln\sigma_k + \beta_7 \ln INF_i + \theta_j + \gamma_k + \tau_t + e_{ijkt} \tag{3}$$

where (i) indexes foreign countries and (j) indexes ports in the importing countries. Accordingly,

$$\frac{F_{ijkt}}{V_{ijkt}}$$

is the ad valorem freight rate of product k transported between country i and port j in year t,

$$\frac{WGT_{ijkt}}{V_{ijkt}}$$

[32] Specifically, the index measures the fraction of the population in a country that has access to an airport with paved runways at least 2000 meters long and 40 meters wide. To account for the "quality" of airport infrastructure, understood as runway availability per million city inhabitants, the authors interact this share of population with the quantity of runways per million inhabitants.

is the weight-to-value ratio of good k, $DIST_{ij}$ is the distance between country i and port j, q_{ijt} is the total volume of imports (in kilograms) carried by ocean between country i and port j, n_{ij} is the number of shippers between country i and port j, λ_{iJkt} is the effective ad valorem tariff that country i faces in country J for good k, σ_k is the elasticity of import demand of good k, INF_i is a proxy for port infrastructure of the exporting country i,[33] θ_j is the set of fixed-effects parameters for each port of entry in the importing countries (this is our measure of port efficiency in the importing country), γ_k is the product fixed effect, and e_{ijkt} is the error term.[34]

The results of this estimation are presented in Table 2.B.3 in Appendix 2.B. We also run an alternative specification that controls for the level of port efficiency of the importing countries not at the port level but at the country level using country fixed effects. Therefore, we drop all the port fixed effects of the importing countries in equation (3) and use country fixed effects instead. The results from this alternative specification are very similar to the ones presented in Table 2.B.3. and are available upon request.

2.A.4. Airfreight Model for Imports

For this model we use the same equation (3) to estimate the determinants of air transport costs. We employ a dataset that combines the air transport charges paid by U.S. imports used in the section "Explaining Differences in the Costs to Export" with similar datasets for Latin American countries put together by ALADI. The countries included in the analysis are Brazil, Chile, Ecuador, Peru and Uruguay, in addition to the United States. Similar to the maritime transport mode, the observations are disaggregated at the country level for the origin of the shipment and at the airport level for its destination.

---

[33] Following Clark et al. (2005) we use a measure of port infrastructure that consists of the number of ports that have lifts with leverage capacity of at least 50 tons (squared) divided by the product of the country population and surface. The information about ports is taken from Portualia.com.

[34] The ALADI dataset does not have information to construct the variables "trade imbalance" or "containerization." Therefore, these two variables do not appear in the specification.

Therefore, the data consists of country-to-airport pairs except for the variables "distance" and the "number of airlines" that are only available at the country-to-country level.[35] The results of this estimation are presented in Table 2.B.4 in Appendix 2.B. [36]

It is worth mentioning that the above specifications can be improved in several aspects. For example, we have treated port and airport efficiency in all the models of this chapter as time-invariant variables. Although factors like the quality of a port infrastructure might not change rapidly over short periods of time, this is an assumption that can be relaxed in future work. Another aspect is the treatment of the tariff rate and the volume of imports. The tariff rate might not only have a direct impact on the ad valorem freight rate, as measured in these regressions, but also an indirect impact through the volume of imports. Quantifying the indirect impact, however, would require the use of a simultaneous equation model, an extension that could be done. We should also mention that some caution should be exercised when interpreting the results from these regressions as some econometric issues are likely to be present. For example, the regressions are subject to exhibit sample selection and potential serial correlation. The sample selection problem usually arises because of the exclusion of country pairs (or port pairs) with zero trade flows (see, e.g., Helpman, Melitz and Rubinstein 2007). Serial correlation tends to be an issue in trade models because trade flows normally display some degree of inertia. Although these problems are not likely to affect significantly the results or the conclusions of this chapter, they might be addressed in future work.

---

[35] The proxy for airport infrastructure of the exporting country is the ratio between the squared number of airports with runways of at least 1500 meters long and the product of the country area and total population.

[36] Once again, we also run an alternative specification that controls for the level of port efficiency of the importing countries not at the port level but at the country level using country fixed effects. The results do not change in any significant way to the ones presented in Table 2.B.4.

Appendix 2.B
Estimation Results

Table 2.B.1. Determinants of Ocean Shipping Costs for Exports

Dependent Variable: Shipping Costs per Value	(1)	(2)
Weight / Value	0.473	0.473
	(.001)***	(.001)***
Distance	0.136	0.136
	(0.007)**	(0.007)**
Volume of Imports	−0.003	−0.003
	(.002)*	(.002)*
Directional Trade Imbalance	−0.156	−0.156
	(.019)***	(.019)***
Containerization	−0.018	−0.018
	(.004)***	(.004)***
Number of Shippers	−0.015	−0.014
	(.003)***	(.003)***
Tariff	0.487	0.486
	(.025)***	(.025)***
Import Demand Elasticity	−0.005	−0.004
	(.001)***	(.001)***
Shippers × Elasticity		−0.001
		(.86)
Constant	−4.333	−4.335
	(0.233)***	(0.233)***
R-squared	0.31	0.31
Observations	1604350	1604350

All regressions include time, commodity and port fixed effects (not shown due to space limitations). *F*-tests confirm that the port fixed effects are jointly significant at 1%.

* Significant at 10%, ** Significant at 5%, *** Significant at 1%.

Table 2.B.2. Determinants of Air Shipping Costs for Exports

Dependent Variable: Shipping Costs per Value	(1)	(2)	(3)
Weight / Value	0.4688	0.4827	0.4711
	(.01)***	(.01)***	(.01)***
Distance	0.1357	0.1577	0.1427
	(0.06)**	(0.07)**	(0.06)**
Import Volume	0.0276	0.0337	0.0152
	(.04)	(.04)	(.04)
Number of Airlines	−0.0507	−0.0444	−0.0389
	(.05)	(.05)	(.05)
Import Demand Elasticity	−0.0124	−0.0137	−0.0128
	(.002)***	(.002)***	(.002)***
Tariff	0.6321	0.3752	0.5553
	(.26)**	(0.32)	(.28)*
Access to Airports Index	−0.1076		−0.1099
	(.02)***		(.03)***
Airport Traffic Divided by Runway Length		−0.0073	−0.0009
		(.01)	(.01)
Constant	−2.3690	−4.1462	−3.6693
	(0.33)***	(0.75)***	(0.58)***
R-squared	0.49	0.48	0.49
Observations	351013	351020	336936

All regressions include time and commodity fixed effects. Import volume is instrumented with GDP (in logs). Cluster robust standard errors in parentheses (by country).

* Significant at 10%, ** Significant at 5%, *** Significant at 1%.

Table 2.B.3. Determinants of Ocean Shipping Costs for Imports

Dependent Variable: Shipping Costs per Value	
Weight / Value	0.4975
	(.008)***
Distance	0.1770
	(0.03)***
Import Volume	−0.0045
	(.01)
Number of Shippers	−0.0356
	(.01)**
Tariff	1.3742
	(.11)***
Import Demand Elasticity	−0.0097
	(.004)**
Foreign Infrastructure	−0.0058
	(.004)
Constant	−5.4710
	(1.48)***
R-squared	0.37
Observations	106160

The estimation is for the year 2005, except data from Ecuador that is for 2004. The regression includes commodity and importer port fixed effects (not shown due to space limitations). An *F*-test confirms that the port fixed effects are jointly significant at 1%. Import volume is instrumented with GDP (in logs). Cluster robust standard errors in parentheses (by country).

* Significant at 10%, ** Significant at 5%, *** Significant at 1%.

Table 2.B.4. Determinants of Air Shipping Costs for Imports

Dependent Variable: Shipping Costs per Value	
Weight / Value	0.5361
	(0.01)***
Distance	0.1687
	(0.07)**
Import Volume	0.0124
	(.02)
Number of Shippers	−0.0418
	(.03)
Tariff	2.1679
	(.15)***
Import Demand Elasticity	−0.0071
	(.002)**
Foreign Infrastructure	−0.0499
	(.01)***
Constant	−1.8259
	(0.47)***
R-squared	0.51
Observations	356179

The estimation is for the year 2005, except data from Ecuador that is for 2004. The regression includes commodity and importer airport fixed effects (not shown due to space limitations). An *F*-test confirms that the airport fixed effects are jointly significant at 1%. Import volume is instrumented with GDP (in logs). Cluster robust standard errors in parentheses (by country).

* Significant at 10%, ** Significant at 5%, *** Significant at 1%.

References

Batista, J. 2007. *Trade Costs for Brazilian Exporting Goods: Two Case Studies.* Washington, D.C.: Inter-American Development Bank.

Blonigen, B., and W. Wilson. 2006. *New Measures of Port Efficiency Using International Trade Data.* Working Paper 12052. Cambridge, MA: National Bureau of Economic Research.

Borenstein, S., and N. Rose. 2007. *How Airline Markets Work... Or Do They? Regulatory Reform in the Airline Industry.* Working Paper 13452. Cambridge, MA: National Bureau of Economic Research.

Broda, C., and D. Weinstein. 2006. Globalization and the Gains from Variety. *Quarterly Journal of Economics* 121(2): 541–585.

Clark, X., D. Dollar and A. Micco. 2005. Port Efficiency, Maritime Transport Costs, and Bilateral Trade. *Journal of Development Economics* 75: 417–450.

Fink, C., A. Mattoo and I. Neagu. 2002 (December). *Trade Effectiveness of Collusion under Anti-Trust Immunity, the Case of Liner Shipping Conferences.* Washington, D.C.: Federal Trade Commission.

Foxley, J., and J. Mardones. 2000. Port Concessions in Chile: Contract Design to Promote Competition and Investment. *Viewpoint: Public Policy for the Private Sector,* Note No. 223. Washington, D.C.: World Bank.

Helpman, E., M. Melitz and Y. Rubinstein. 2007. *Estimating Trade Flows: Trading Partners and Trading Volumes.* Working Paper 12927. Cambridge, MA: National Bureau of Economic Research.

Heston, A., R. Summers and B. Aten. 2006 (September). *Penn World Table Version 6.2.* Pittsburgh: University of Pennsylvania Center for International Comparisons of Production, Income and Prices.

Hoffman, J. 2000. *Tendencias en el Transporte Marítimo Internacional y sus Implicaciones para América Latina y el Caribe.* Santiago, Chile: Economic Commission for Latin America and the Caribbean.

Hummels, D. 2001. Toward a Geography of Trade Costs. West Lafayette, IN: Purdue University, mimeo.

Hummels, D., V. Lugovskyy and A. Skiba. Forthcoming. The Trade Reducing Effects of Market Power in International Shipping. *Journal of Development Economics.*

Micco, A., and T. Serebrisky. 2006. Competition Regimes and Air Transport Costs: The Effects of Open Skies Agreements. *Journal of International Economics* 70: 25–51.

Ricover, A., and E. Negre. 2004. *Estudio de Integración del Transporte Aéreo en Sudamérica.* Washington, D.C.: Inter-American Development Bank.

Sicra, R. 2007. *Costos de Exportación en Argentina, Dos Casos de Estudio.* Washington, D.C.: Inter-American Development Bank.

Trujillo, L., and A. Estache. 2001. Surfing a Wave of Fine Tuning Reforms in Argentina's Ports. Washington, D.C.: World Bank, mimeo.

Vega, H. 2007. Transportation Costs of Fresh Flowers: A Comparison across Major Exporting Countries. Washington, D.C.: Inter-American Development Bank.

Wilmsmeier, G., J. Hoffman and R. Sanchez. 2006. The Impact of Port Characteristics on International Maritime Transport Costs. In *Port Economics,* ed. K. Cullinane and W. Talley. New York: Elsevier.

World Economic Forum. 2005. *Global Competitiveness Report 2005–2006.* Geneva: World Economic Forum.

———. 2007. *Global Competitiveness Report 2007–2008.* Geneva: World Economic Forum.

CHAPTER 3

Transport Costs, Tariffs and the Volume and Diversification of the Region's Trade

In the previous chapters, we were focused on assessing the level of transport costs in the region and its determinants. We learned that, for both quantitative and strategic reasons, transport costs are a more important obstacle to LAC's trade than tariffs and we also learned that a government agenda centered on bringing transport costs down should have among its priorities the improvement of ports and airports, the promotion of competition in the shipping industry and the further lowering of import tariffs. We have not discussed in any detail, though, what would be the impact of such an agenda on the volume and diversification of the region's trade. For instance, we have argued that improving port efficiency to the level of a country such as the United States would reduce ocean freight on average by 20 percent, but what about the impact on trade? What would such improvements mean to the volume of goods the region imports and exports? What would they mean for the variety of goods the region trades?

This chapter addresses these questions. More concretely, it aims at analyzing the impact, over the last decade, of transport costs on the trade flows of nine Latin American countries—Argentina, Bolivia, Brazil, Chile, Colombia, Ecuador, Paraguay, Peru, and Uruguay—where the full data on freight rates is available.[37] We assess how these costs affect both sectoral import and export volumes and how they shape trade diversification patterns across countries and compare their relative importance with that of a key trade policy barrier, tariffs.

[37] We use the ALADI database, which provides us with highly disaggregated trade and trade costs data for the following countries: Argentina, Bolivia, Brazil, Chile, Colombia, Ecuador, Paraguay, Peru, and Uruguay.

The analysis of the impact of transport costs on trade is particularly opportune at a time when most LAC countries lag behind both in terms of their engagement in international trade and the degree of diversification of their trade relationships. For instance, the LAC countries in our sample have levels of imports and exports below those that could be expected according to their economic sizes and level of development (see Figures 3.1 and 3.2). Moreover, they rank relatively low in terms of exports and imports per capita (Table 3.1). With the exception of Chile, these rankings have been worsening over recent years along with the stagnation and even decline of the subregion's shares of world trade, despite the extraordinarily favorable prices for its main export products (Figure 3.3).

The degree of diversification of these countries' export bundles is also in general smaller than could be predicted from their sizes (see Figure 3.4) and below or just about average in terms of their development levels (see, e.g., Cadot et al. 2007). The extensive margin of their exports, that is, the new products introduced over recent years, is almost exclusively concentrated in products with low degree of differentiation (see Cadot et al. 2007). Can transport costs be one of the factors contributing to explain this trade performance below expectations? Or to put it differently, can lower transport costs help to reverse this situation? By estimating the impact of trade costs on trade, this chapter provides some precise answers to these questions.

Trade Costs and Trade Patterns

The easiest and standard way to model trade costs, in general, and transport costs, in particular, is to assume that these costs are ad valorem and that they are met by the wastage of a proportion of the goods traded. This is called the "iceberg" trade cost assumption as goods are seen as melting down in transit (see, e.g., Samuelson 1954; Mundell 1957; Krugman 1980, 1991). Appendix 3.A presents an explanation of this concept using a diagrammatic approach.

This modeling strategy has several advantages and, accordingly, has reasons to prevail (see Hummels and Skiba 2004a). The most important advantage lies in the assumption that firms charge the same FOB (free on board) prices in all markets and apply a common trade factor cost across

Figure 3.1 Total Trade and Economic Size

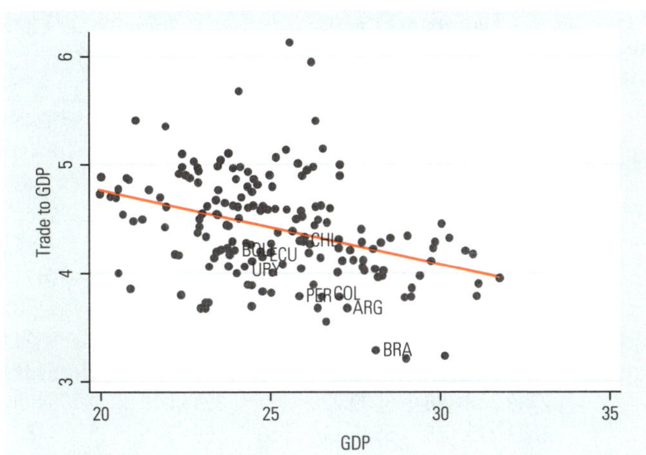

Figure 3.2 Exports and Level of Development

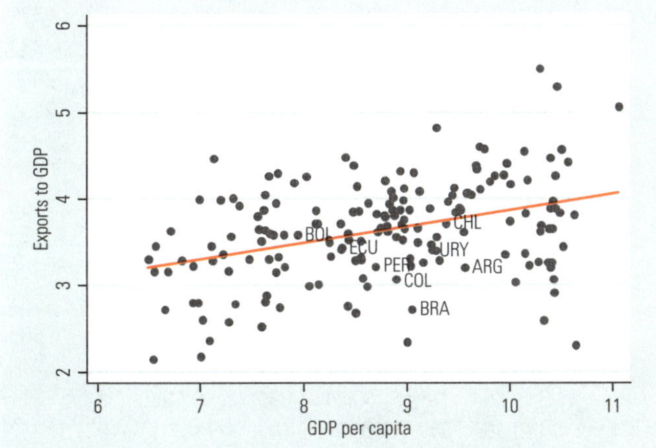

The figures present the (natural logarithm of the) ratio of total trade to GDP against (the natural logarithm of) GDP (in PPP terms) and the (natural logarithm of the) ratio of exports to GDP against (the natural logarithm of) GDP per capita (in PPP terms), respectively, for all countries with information using data for 2005 or the latest available year from the *World Development Indicators* (World Bank various years).

Table 3.1

Selected Countries	Exports per Capita				Imports per Capita			
	1995		2005		1995		2005	
Singapore	33480.627	1	52717.191	1	35219.829	1	45848.617	1
Ireland	12133.871	3	26446.522	6	8951.840	7	16900.878	7
Finland	7905.358	9	12425.789	15	5777.154	16	11143.401	15
Germany	6217.427	17	11838.128	16	5412.049	19	9442.318	20
Canada	6440.061	16	11035.462	17	5582.177	18	9665.283	19
Slovenia	4178.335	21	9639.666	19	4767.349	22	10171.838	18
Czech Republic	2097.161	35	7640.592	22	2447.340	39	7476.413	28
United Kingdom	4019.167	23	6381.991	25	4485.902	24	8564.040	22
Hungary	1205.187	41	6172.782	28	1470.192	48	6534.953	31
Korea	2719.388	28	5889.289	31	2935.610	34	5409.260	41
Malaysia	3621.273	25	5545.218	33	3691.175	28	4466.797	44
Australia	2716.891	29	4983.505	35	3147.437	33	5744.885	40
Japan	3528.177	26	4645.080	37	2653.432	38	4026.837	48
Spain	2270.970	33	4440.667	38	2870.512	37	6661.734	29
United States	2170.161	34	3032.271	43	2886.709	36	5829.370	38
Chile	1078.860	43	2347.822	44	1035.296	58	1832.279	68
Poland	592.258	63	2341.534	45	751.993	69	2660.284	53
Mexico	870.880	49	2074.752	48	794.324	68	2150.517	60
Romania	348.752	72	1281.739	63	453.150	77	1870.308	65
Argentina	601.768	62	1031.404	67	577.628	74	740.406	90
Turkey	349.814	71	1017.691	68	578.378	73	1566.355	72
Uruguay	652.904	57	1016.894	69	890.483	62	1173.384	79
Ecuador	374.295	69	744.631	76	368.071	81	726.368	91
Brazil	285.949	76	633.405	80	332.972	83	394.841	113
China	123.483	96	584.096	83	109.626	106	505.905	102
Peru	208.785	85	502.084	87	318.156	87	446.999	107
Colombia	262.094	78	457.513	90	362.885	82	471.772	105
Bolivia	140.397	94	296.098	102	185.414	98	253.270	119
Paraguay	191.569	88	286.137	104	653.449	72	629.793	94

This table presents exports and imports per capita for selected countries for 1995 and 2005 computed using data from the World Bank's *World Development Indicators*. Countries are ranked according to exports per capita, in decreasing order.

goods. In this setting, transport costs do not change relative prices, and, therefore, relative demands are not affected.[38] Moreover, by assuming that

[38] This implies assuming away quality responses and pricing to market. The latter effect is less important when markets are more competitive and products are not differentiated across destinations. We thank David Hummels for pointing this out.

Figure 3.3 South America in World Trade

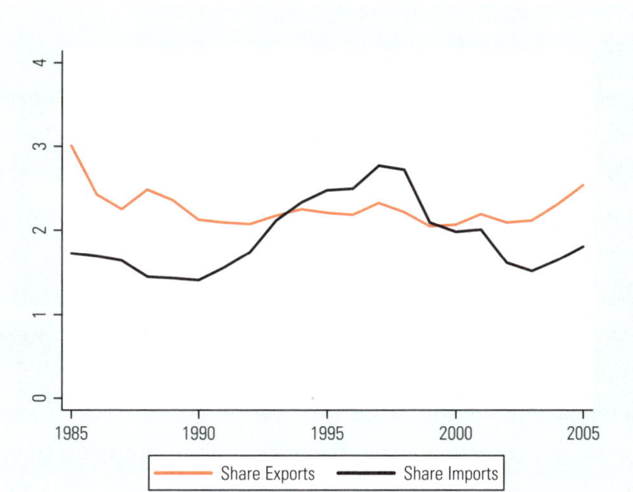

Figure 3.4 Export Diversification and Economic Size

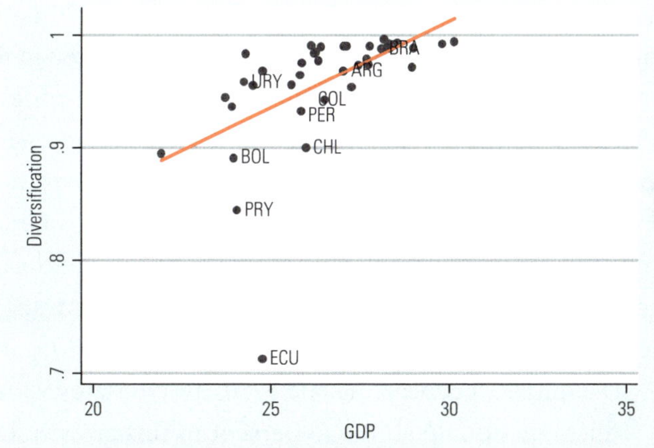

Figure 3.3 shows the percentage share of our sample countries, i.e., South American countries (except for Venezuela) in world imports and exports using data from COMTRADE, while Figure 3.4 presents the complement of the Herfindahl index of export concentration computed on SITC 4-digit level data against (the natural logarithm of) GDP (in PPP terms) using data for 2005 or the latest available year from COMTRADE and the *World Development Indicators* (World Bank various years).

trade costs take the form of a fraction of goods that disappear in transit, there is no need to deal with the problems arising when a transport industry is explicitly considered.[39]

In reality, though, transport costs have not only a *per value*, but also a *per unit* component. Therefore, transport costs can alter relative prices and accordingly relative demands across quality segments. In particular, they may be positively related to goods' prices. This positive correlation can be traced back to insurance charges, more costly handling requirements for high-quality goods or the need to rely on more expensive transportation modes such as air shipping, or may reflect successful monopoly power exercised by transportation firms (see Hummels and Skiba 2004a).

Several papers in the empirical international trade literature have aimed at explicitly measuring the effect of transport costs on trade. Most of these studies assume ad valorem costs. Geraci and Prewo (1977), for instance, estimate transport cost elasticities for a set of member countries of the Organisation for Economic Co-operation and Development (OECD), using cross-sectional data of aggregated bilateral trade flows for 1970, and find that these elasticities range from 0.19 in the case of Belgium to 2.60 in the case of Australia. Harrigan (1993) focuses on a similar sample of countries, but with data for 1983, and concludes that transport costs and tariffs were a more substantial barrier to trade in manufactures between developed countries than were non-tariff barriers. Moreover, he shows that transport costs and tariffs seemed to have significantly different effects for most industries.

Baier and Bergstrand (2001), in turn, show that transport cost declines account for about 8 percent of the growth of world trade among several OECD countries between the late 1950s and the late 1980s, whereas tariff-rate reductions explain about 25 percent of this growth. Using data for a large set of developing and developed countries for 1990, Limao and Venables (2001) estimate an elasticity of trade flows with respect to transport costs of approximately 2.5, which means that halving transport costs would increase the volume of trade by a factor of five. Finally, De

---

[39] Formally, transportation technology is implicitly assumed to be identical to the technology for producing goods. More specifically, the capital-labor ratio employed in the transport industry is confined to lie within those used in the other industries (see Falvey 1976).

(2006) provides evidence on the role of transport costs in northeast Asia. He shows that transaction costs and trade infrastructure facilities have a significant influence on trade flows in this region.

Even though all these papers present valuable insights on the impact of transport costs on trade, the evidence they report can at most be considered suggestive. The reason is that these studies share a major weakness, namely, none of them has used actual transport cost data at the product level.[40] They just resort to aggregate proxies at the country level, in most cases the difference between FOB values reported by the exporter country and CIF values reported by the corresponding importer country.[41] Thus, these data do not account for the compositional shifts in aggregate trade flows over time.

Furthermore, the level of aggregate freight expenditures may endogenously result from transport cost minimizing decisions, thus being relatively low. This is in fact what the data suggest. When compared to actual disaggregated freight rates, these aggregate indicators are at the low end of the distribution and thus are likely to understate the shipping costs borne in international trade. Finally, a high proportion of the aggregate bilateral CIF/FOB ratios is imputed.[42] Using these data as a measure of transport costs is therefore at least questionable (see Hummels 2001; Anderson and van Wincoop 2004; and Hummels and Lugovskyy 2006).

One notable exception in this literature is the paper by Hummels (2001), who estimates the effect of trade barriers on trade flows for 62 two-digit SITC (Standard International Trade Classification) "goods" using highly disaggregated trade and freight and tariff rate data (i.e., at the

---

[40] An exception is Clark, Dollar and Micco (2004), who investigate the determinants of shipping costs to the United States using transport cost data at the product level. From these estimates they derive country-specific maritime transport indexes that they include as an explanatory variable in a standard aggregated gravity equation. They find that port efficiency is an important explanatory factor of these costs and that reducing countries' inefficiencies associated with transport costs from the 25th to the 75th percentile would increase bilateral trade around 25 percent.

[41] Beckerman (1956) and Balassa (1961) suggested for the first time using the difference between CIF and FOB values as an indicator of "economic distance" (see Geraci and Prewo 1977).

[42] Geraci and Prewo (1997) acknowledge that the differences between CIF and FOB values are inaccurate measures of transport costs and therefore apply an errors-in-variables approach when estimating their impact on trade flows.

five-digit SITC level) for 1992 on the United States, New Zealand, Argentina, Brazil, Chile, Paraguay, and Uruguay. He reports an average elasticity of 5.6 implying in this case that a 10 percent increase in transport costs or tariffs lowers trade by 56 percent.[43]

Unlike previous studies, Hummels and Skiba (2004a) assume that, instead of being strictly ad valorem, transport costs have a per unit component. Using data for Argentina, Brazil, Chile, Paraguay, Uruguay, and the United States for 1994 at the six-digit Harmonized System (HS) level, these authors find that exporters charge destination-varying FOB prices that covariate positively with shipping costs (and negatively with ad valorem tariffs). The share of high- relative to low-quality goods in the import bundle then increases with per unit freight. This suggests that transport costs lead firms to ship high-quality goods abroad holding low-quality goods for domestic consumption.

New Evidence on Latin America: Preliminaries

To examine the impact of transport costs vis-à-vis tariffs on sectoral trade and trade diversification across countries in the region, we make use of a broad dataset, both in terms of country coverage and time span. It consists of highly disaggregated import data (6-digit HS) on transport costs (freight plus insurance) and real tariffs (import revenue divided by imports) for nine Latin American countries (Argentina, Bolivia, Brazil, Chile, Colombia, Ecuador, Paraguay, Peru, Uruguay) and the United States, for the years 1995 and 2000–2005.[44] The 6-digit "products" are grouped into 2-digit

---

[43] Martínez-Zarzoso and Suárez-Burguet (2005) assess the effect of transport costs on Latin American imports from the European Union using similar data for 1998, but a higher level of aggregation, i.e., three-digit SITC level.

[44] There are some observations for which transport costs and tariffs exceed the amount traded. In our benchmark estimations, we have dropped these observations, which in most cases correspond to extremely small trade flows (e.g., US$10). Robustness exercises redefining the sample used in the econometric analysis have been performed and their results are reported in Appendix 3.D. Table 3.D.1 in Appendix 3.D identifies, for each year, the countries for which data on all three variables are available. The first six digits of the HS classification are common across countries. Data is also reported at the five-digit SITC, Revision 2. Results using this level of aggregation are similar to those reported below and will therefore not be presented. They are available from the authors upon request.

sectors (chapters) and these two into broader categories namely, agriculture, mineral and metals, and manufacturing.[45]

Countries of origin are all actual trading partners around the world. Hence, when looking at imports, all flows will be covered, whereas when looking at exports, only exports to those countries for which we have data on imports, namely, those listed above, will be taken into account. We also have data on distance between countries' capitals and indicators of contiguity and common language from the Centre d'études prospectives et d'informations internationales (CEPII) database (see the Data Appendix).[46]

One key issue for the analysis is the measurement of the different components of trade costs. We measure transport costs as the ratio of freight plus insurance to trade values and tariffs as actually collected tariff revenues divided by trade value.[47]

Figures 3.5 and 3.6 present a first visual representation of the relationship between trade costs and two key trade indicators—sectoral imports and number of products exported—using data at the six-digit HS level for 2005. Figure 3.5 shows the relationship between (the natural logarithm of) sectoral imports for all countries in the sample from all possible origins and (the natural logarithm of one plus) freight and tariff rates as

[45] Conventionally, empirical analyses consider that agriculture covers chapters 1–24, while manufacturing covers the remaining ones. Given that many countries in the region are highly specialized either in minerals or metals and their related products, we have decided to open a new category to group goods from these sectors. Concretely, we define chapters 1–24 as agriculture, chapters 25–27 and 68–83 as minerals and metals, and the remaining chapters as manufacturing.

[46] Common border (common language) is a binary variable taking the value of one if the importer and the exporter countries share a border (at least 9 percent of the population of the importer and the exporter countries speak the same language) and zero otherwise.

[47] A second important issue is the interaction between the different components of trade costs. Most studies assume a multiplicative trade cost function, that is, total trade costs are represented as the product of several component costs that are captured by proxy variables. This has the odd economic implication that the marginal effect of a change in one cost hinges upon all other costs (see Hummels 2001). Alternatively, trade cost components can be combined additively. Here, we adopt the latter specification and measure explicit trade costs as the sum of freight (and insurance) and tariff rates.

Figure 3.5. Trade Costs and Sectoral Imports

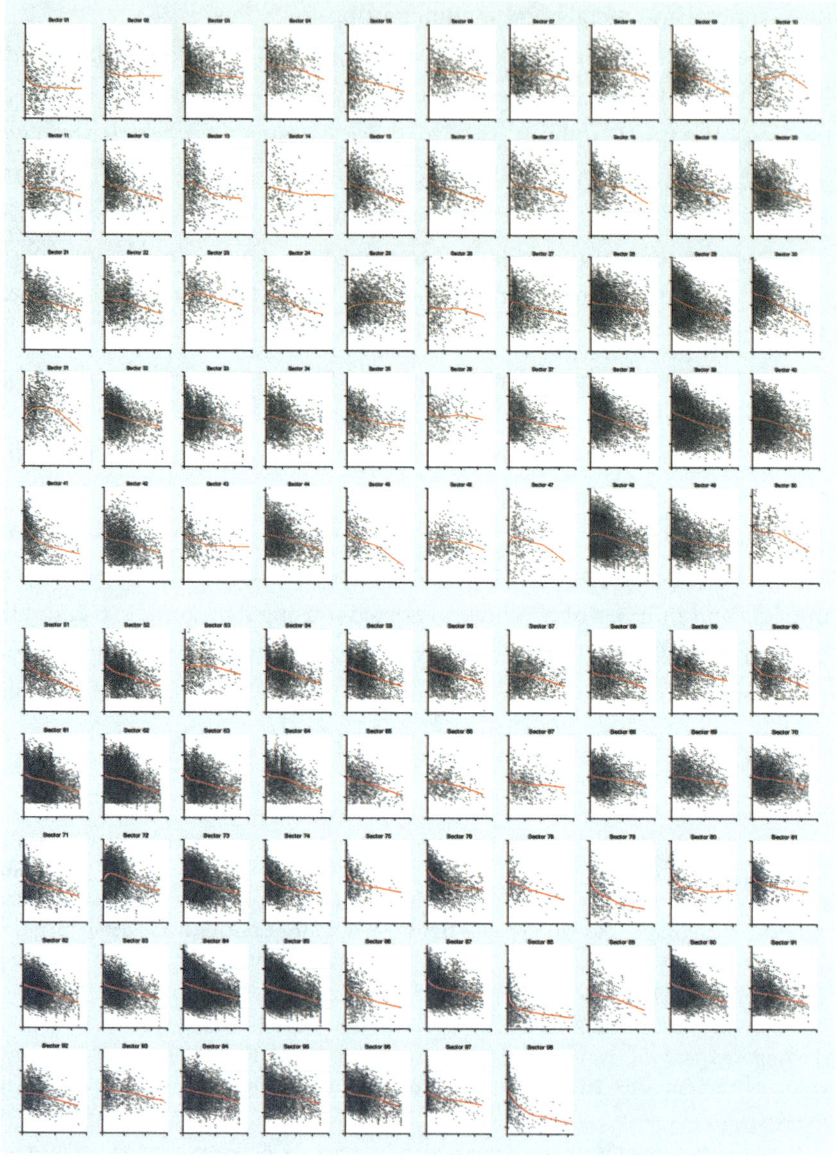

The figure shows the relationship between (the natural logarithm of) bilateral imports at the product level for each sector (vertical axis) and the corresponding trade costs as measured by (the natural logarithm of one plus) the ratio of freight and insurance plus tariff revenue to trade (horizontal axis), after controlling for (time-invariant) country-specific characteristics.

Figure 3.6. Trade Costs and Export Diversification

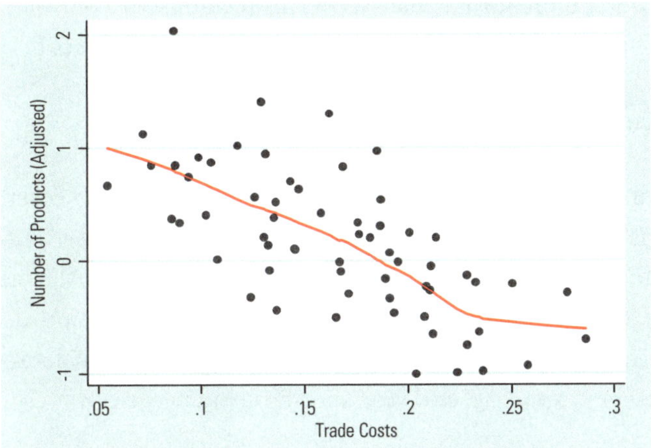

The figure shows the relationship between (the natural logarithm of) the number of products exported by each country to each partner in the sample (vertical axis) and the corresponding average trade costs (horizontal axis), after controlling for (time-invariant) country-specific characteristics.

defined above. Figure 3.6, in turn, presents the relationship between (the natural logarithm of) the number of products exported by each country to each pair in the sample and the aforementioned measure of trade costs evaluated at the mean freight and tariff rates.[48] In both cases, we control for exporter- and importer-specific characteristics.[49]

As can be seen, the relationship between trade costs and both sectoral trade and trade diversification is clearly negative in most cases. More specifically, as highlighted by Figure 3.5, the intensity of the link between sectoral trade and trade costs varies substantially across sectors, which clearly

---

[48] More precisely, Figures 3.5 and 3.6 display both a simple scatterplot and robust locally weighted scatterplot smoothing, i.e., *lowess*. The *lowess* consists of running a regression of trade flows (trade diversification) on trade costs for each observation using a small amount of data around them. The fitted value of this regression evaluated at each value taken by trade costs is then used as a smoothed value to construct the non-parametric curve linking these variables. For additional descriptions of this non-parametric method see Cleveland (1979) and Goodall (1990) and for a recent application see Imbs and Wacziarg (2003).

[49] Formally, we net out these country specificities by regressing the natural logarithm of the trade variables on importer and exporter fixed effects and taking the residuals.

indicates that this link should be explored at this level. In the next section, we carry out a more formal analysis of this relationship, controlling for the potential influence of other factors on trade volume and diversification.

Empirical Assessment

The empirical approach used to assess the impact of trade costs on trade patterns is based on a multi-sector model. The formal derivation of the relationships to be estimated can be found in Appendix 3.C. These equations suggest that bilateral trade and bilateral diversification depend on bilateral trade costs, as defined in the previous section, bilateral distance, and importer-, exporter-, and year-specific characteristics.

Trade Costs and Sectoral Bilateral Trade

The bilateral trade equations are first estimated pooling over all products (i.e., 6-digit HS), but controlling for product-specific characteristics, to get an approximate average measure of the effect of trade costs on trade flows.[50] This is shown schematically in Table 3.2, where bilateral trade costs are defined as one plus the ratio of freight and insurance plus tariffs to trade values, and imports, exports, trade costs and distance are expressed in natural logarithms.

As shown in the theoretical model (Appendix 3.C), since goods have different characteristics that affect their transportability, trade cost effects

Table 3.2

Determinants of Bilateral Imports/Exports at the Product Level
Bilateral Trade Costs at the Product Level (−)
Bilateral Distance (−)
Permanent Importer-Specific Characteristics
Permanent Exporter-Specific Characteristics
Permanent Product-Specific Characteristics

Note: Expected signs are between parentheses.

---

[50] Formally, these characteristics are controlled for by fixed effects. Reported estimates are based on the specification including importer, exporter, and year fixed effects. Unless otherwise stated, these will be the default specifications. Those regressions including time-varying importer and exporter yield qualitatively the same results.

Table 3.3

For Each Sector: Determinants of Bilateral Imports/Exports at the Product Level
Bilateral Trade Costs at the Product Level (−)
Bilateral Distance (−)
Permanent Importer-Specific Characteristics
Permanent Exporter-Specific Characteristics

Note: Expected signs are between parentheses.

on trade are likely to differ across sectors, which is consistent with the type of results we saw in Figure 3.5. We, therefore, estimate (see Table 3.3) the equations sector by sector, that is, pooling over all products within each sector (i.e., 2-digit HS).[51]

Tables 3.D.1 to 3.D.4 in Appendix 3.D report the estimation results when pooling across all goods, while Figures 3.7 and 3.8 present direct visual representations of the estimated sectoral impacts along with the corresponding estimated distributions, for both imports and exports.[52]

The average impact of trade costs on bilateral imports, as estimated in fully pooled regressions, and the corresponding average and median impacts, when estimated at the sectoral level (see Figure 3.7), suggest that a 10 percent reduction in trade costs would lead approximately to a 50 percent expansion of bilateral imports.[53] It is worth noting that there is a significant variation across sectors. The estimated effect of such a decrease in trade costs ranges from 5.5 percent in the case of salt, sulfur and stones (Sector 26) to 96.6 percent in the case of articles of leather (Sector 42), with no sectors registering values that are not statistically significantly different

[51] This implies assuming that the effect of trade costs is symmetric across goods within sectors. Since we are mainly interested in the impact of these costs on trade volumes and trade diversification as measured by the number of products traded instead of in their effect on the quality composition of trade, we assume that trade costs are ad valorem. For more details see Appendix 3.C.

[52] Formally, we present kernel densities estimated using the Epanechnikov kernel with automatic optimal bandwidth selection (see Silverman 1986).

[53] In most cases, estimates including and excluding the United States are similar to each other. Further, this estimated average impact seems to be robust to changes in sample and inclusion of additional control variables (see Tables 3.D.2 and 3.D.3). In this regard, notice that sharing a border and having a common language raise bilateral trade flows. The effect of trade costs seems to be relatively constant over time (see Table 3.D.4).

Figure 3.7. Impact of Trade Costs on Sectoral Imports

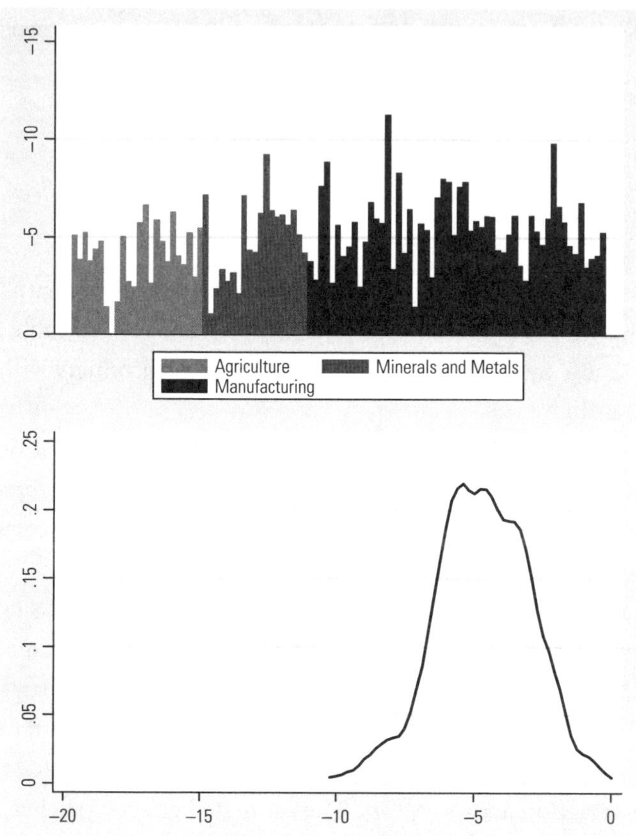

The figure presents the impact of trade costs on sectoral imports as estimated at the product level (6-digit HS) pooling at the sector level (2-digit HS) (top) and the share distribution of these sectoral impacts over their levels (bottom), based on the specification including importer, exporter, and year fixed effects and excluding the United States. Within broad sectors (agriculture, minerals and metals, and manufacturing), observations are correlatively ordered according to the respective 2-digit HS.

from zero. More generally, the average increase of bilateral imports induced by a 10 percent decline of trade costs would be larger for manufacturing (48.4 percent) than for minerals and metals (47.1 percent) and agricultural products (42.9 percent).[54] Among these products, the largest impact

[54] The corresponding median values are 46.8 percent, 52.5 percent, and 38.3 percent, respectively.

Figure 3.8. Impact of Trade Costs on Sectoral Exports

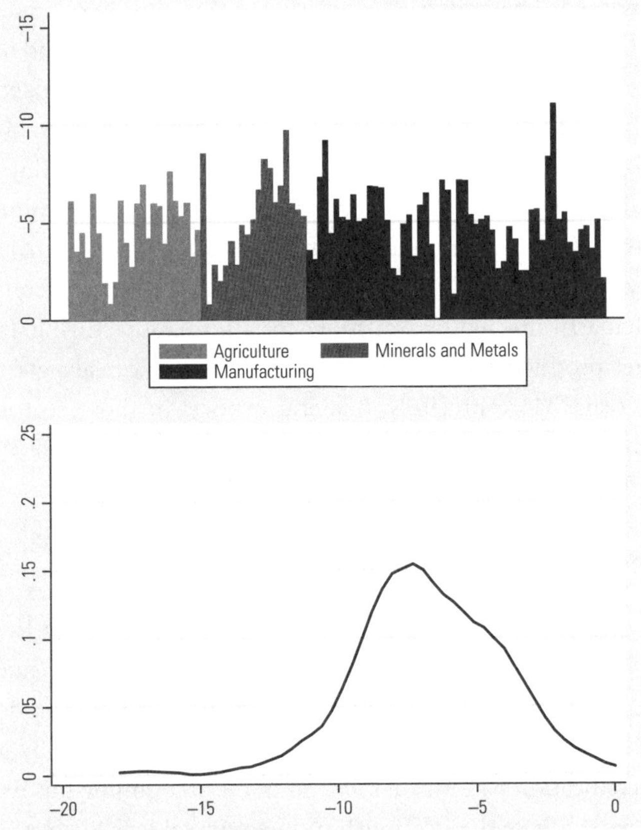

The figure presents the impact of trade costs on sectoral exports as estimated at the product level (6-digit HS) pooling at the sector level (2-digit HS) (top) and the share distribution of these sectoral impacts over their levels (bottom), based on the specification including importer, exporter, and year fixed effects and excluding the United States. Within broad sectors (agriculture, minerals and metals, and manufacturing), observations are correlatively ordered according to the respective 2-digit HS.

is 64.7 percent and corresponds to preparations of cereals. Furthermore, dispersion across sectors is smallest in agriculture and manufacturing.

The average impact of trade costs on bilateral exports, as emerging from the pooled estimation, and the corresponding average and median impact over the 2-digit sectors (see Figure 3.8, above) indicate that reducing trade costs by 10 percent would result in an increase of (intraregional) bilateral exports of the LAC countries in the sample of larger than

60 percent. As with the case of imports, a substantial variation across sectors is observed. The largest effect of such a diminution of trade costs is found in tin and articles thereof (Sector 80) (169.2 percent) and the smallest in salt, sulfur and stones (Sector 26) (3.6 percent). The impact of trade costs on bilateral exports is statistically different from zero in all sectors. On average, the expansion associated with a 10 percent decline of trade costs would be larger for manufacturing (66.3 percent) and minerals and metals (69.2 percent) than for agricultural products (54 percent).[55] Again, variability across sectors is smaller in manufacturing and agriculture. Sectors particularly affected by transport costs in manufacturing are cotton and leather products, while those in agriculture are cereals and preparation of cereals. More precisely, bilateral exports in those sectors would increase by 130 percent, 108.8 percent, 97.1 percent, and 82.3 percent, respectively, if trade costs were lowered 10 percent.

Trade Costs and Bilateral Trade Diversification

As we have seen, the effect of trade costs on both imports and exports is far from being symmetric across sectors and, therefore, we can assume that they also have an impact on the composition of LAC's trade. If they play a role on composition, one can logically expect that they also help shape diversification patterns in bilateral trade. To examine this issue more precisely, we estimate the relationship shown in Table 3.4, where, for both exports and imports, diversification is measured by the number of products traded as determined by counting the number of tariff lines at the six-digit HS level that register positive trade flows for each pair of countries.

The results obtained when estimating these relationships confirm that trade costs also seem to have a significant impact on trade diversification (see Tables 3.D.5 to 3.D.7 in Appendix 3.D). The more conservative estimates suggest that a 10 percent decline in average transport costs would be associated with a 9 percent increase in the number of products imported and with an expansion of more than 10 percent in the number of products exported to the region. Given the diversification patterns observed in 2005, this implies,

---

[55] The corresponding median values are 68.6 percent, 66.7 percent, and 49.9 percent, respectively.

Table 3.4

Determinants of Bilateral Imports/Exports Diversification
Bilateral Trade Costs (−)
Bilateral Distance (−)
Permanent Importer-Specific Characteristics
Permanent Exporter-Specific Characteristics

Note: Expected signs are between parentheses.

for example, that, on average, Argentina would increase in 210 the number of products exported to other LAC countries, whereas the same figure for Brazil, Colombia and Peru would be 253, 53 and 51 products, respectively.

We have seen that trade costs, in general, and transport costs, in particular, have a substantial trade deterring effect, both overall and on the extensive margin. Two natural questions arise: How much would each LAC country gain in terms of increased trade volumes and enhanced export diversification? What would generate the larger gains: lower transport costs or lower tariffs?

How Much Would LAC Countries Benefit from Lower Transport Costs?

To answer these questions, we perform a simple exercise. Using the results of the estimations discussed earlier, we compute how much intraregional bilateral sectoral export volumes and intraregional bilateral export diversification would change if either transport costs or tariffs were reduced by 10 percent.[56] Results of this computation are shown in Figures 3.9 and 3.10. These figures show the median predicted percentage change of exports across sectors and that of the number of products exported across trade partners as a consequence of a 10 percent reduction in transport costs vs. those associated with a 10 percent reduction in tariffs. The main message is robust across countries. A given reduction in transport costs would have

[56] More precisely, we compare the predicted values from the estimations for 2004 with those simulated values that result from assuming that transport costs and tariffs are 10 percent lower. In doing this, given that this reduction is applied on one plus the respective trade costs, a lower bound of one is set on this value. We use 2004 as a benchmark to maximize the number of countries covered in the exercise (see Table 3.B.1 in Appendix 3.B). Accordingly, in this exercise we assume that all other conditions remain as they were in 2004.

Figure 3.9. Reductions in Transport Costs and Tariffs and Median Response of Sectoral Exports

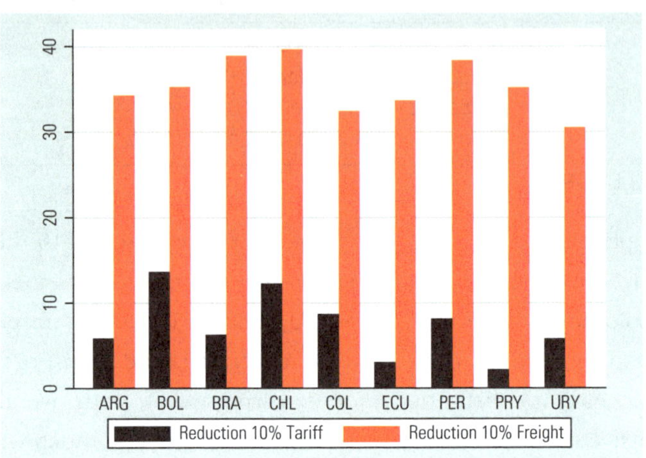

The figure shows the median predicted percentage change of exports across sectors as a consequence of a 10 percent reduction in transport costs and a 10 percent reduction in tariffs for selected Latin American countries, as computed using estimation results from the specification including importer, exporter, and year fixed effect and excluding the United States, and taking 2004 as a benchmark. Exporter countries are on the horizontal axis.

a much larger positive impact on export volumes than a similar reduction in tariffs.[57] This result is hardly surprising given, on the one hand, the significant progress made by LAC countries in terms of intraregional trade liberalization over the last two decades and, on the other, the still substantial gaps in terms of infrastructure investments, especially those linked to cross-border, trade-related projects, which involve substantial coordination problems (see, e.g., Calderón and Servén 2004).

---

[57] We have simulated the effects also for imports for all countries in the sample. While for Bolivia (where transport costs are very high) and Chile (where tariffs are very low) a given reduction in transport costs has a significantly larger impact on sectoral imports than a similar decline in tariffs, the pattern is mixed for the remaining countries. The difference in patterns observed between exports and imports can be explained by the fact that tariffs applied on extraregional trade are substantially larger than those in force in intraregional trade, so that their relative importance as trade deterring factors can be expected to increase vis-à-vis transport costs when all trading partners around the world are considered instead of just regional partners. This is precisely what happens when we estimate the effect of trade costs on imports. These results are available from the authors upon request.

Figure 3.10. Reductions in Transport Costs and Tariffs and Median Response of Export Diversification

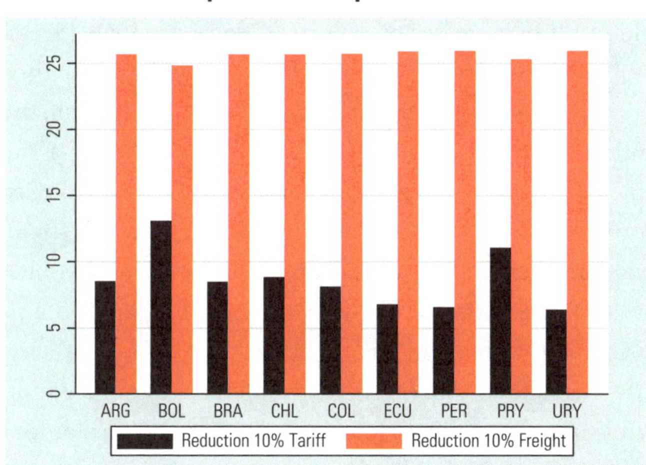

The figure shows the median predicted percentage change of the number of products exported across trade partners as a consequence of a 10 percent reduction in transport costs and a 10 percent reduction in tariffs for selected Latin American countries, as computed using estimation results from the specification including importer, exporter, and year fixed effect and excluding the United States, and taking 2004 as a benchmark. Exporter countries are on the horizontal axis.

Disaggregated estimates indicate that in Brazil, Chile, Colombia, Ecuador, and Uruguay, the average percentage increase of exports that would be induced by lowered transport costs would be the highest in manufacturing.[58] On the other hand, for Argentina, the largest average expansion would be observed in minerals and metals, while in Bolivia, Paraguay, and Peru it would be in agricultural products. However, in most countries, there is significant variation across sectors within each group of activities and accordingly it is difficult to identify a robust cross-grouping pattern.

To illustrate the magnitude of the difference between the predicted impact of reductions in transport costs and that of tariffs, let us consider some particular sectors. Specifically, we look at those sectors/countries

---

[58] Figures reporting sectorally disaggregated predictions are available from the authors upon request.

that are examined in-depth in the case studies that are part of this report (see Chapter 4). Thus, in Argentina, a 10 percent reduction in transport costs would result in increases of exports of dairy products (Sector 4) and machinery (Sector 84) that would be, respectively, 2 and 27 times larger than that derived from a 10 percent decline in tariffs. In Brazil, the impact of an identical cut in transport costs would exceed that of a similar cut in tariffs by a factor of 33, in oil seeds and oleaginous fruits (Sector 12), and 32 in machinery (Sector 84). Figures are even more extreme in the case of Ecuador, where a 10 percent drop in transport costs would increase exports of cut flowers (Sector 6) by 15 percent compared to a negligible impact of a similar decrease in tariffs.

Figure 3.10 shows that, even with differences across countries, the same conclusion we have drawn for sectoral exports also holds for bilateral export diversification, namely, a given reduction of transport costs would lead to a larger expansion of the extensive margin of exports than an equivalent decline in tariffs. The difference between the expected impacts across trading partners is notorious for Peru and Uruguay.

Figure 3.11 highlights that the impact would be even larger if, instead of a simple 10 percent reduction, transport costs for each product were brought down to the lowest level by unit of distance among the Latin American countries in the sample.[59] Sectoral estimates suggest that average exports of manufactured products would rise more than 40 percent in most countries in the region. In particular, the increase would exceed 50 percent in the cases of Peru (56 percent), Bolivia (58 percent), Ecuador (67 percent), Paraguay (88 percent), and Uruguay (104 percent).

At the sectoral level, and using again those sectors/countries focused on by the case studies, exports of dairy products and machinery would

[59] More precisely, for each country and each product we calculate the transport costs per unit of distance across all trading partners. We then pick up the minimum one for each product over all pairs involving countries in the region and apply this value to all bilateral product trade flows to get the expected level of bilateral exports at the product level under this scenario. We finally aggregate across partners and products to obtain sectoral exports and compare these volumes with those estimated under the actual transport costs structure. The figure reports the percentage differences of the aforementioned values. We should stress that this exercise aims at suggesting the potential for enhanced trade that exists if transport costs are lowered. There will be of course cases for which the minimum transport costs in the sample could not be reached due to, for example, geographical conditions.

Figure 3.11. Minimum Transport Cost and Median Sectoral Export Responses

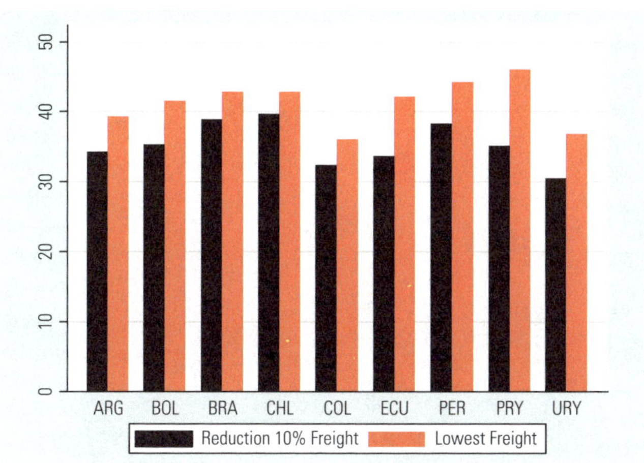

The figure shows the median predicted percentage change in exports across sectors as a consequence of a reduction in transport costs to the lowest level per unit of distance in the sample for selected Latin American countries, as computed using estimation results from the specification including importer, exporter, and year fixed effect and excluding the United States, and taking 2004 as a benchmark. Exporter countries are on the horizontal axis.

increase by 44 percent and 45 percent, respectively, in Argentina; exports of oil seeds and oleaginous fruits and machinery would expand by 57 percent and 48 percent, respectively, in Brazil; and exports of cut flowers would rise about 62 percent in Ecuador.

Finally, in Figures 3.12 and 3.13, we present the results of similar exercises for the volume and diversification of LAC exports to the United States.[60] It is evident that the patterns previously detected in intraregional trade also prevail in this case. Transport costs have a much stronger effect on trade volumes and trade diversification than tariffs. The ratio of the effects of transport costs on export volumes to those of tariffs has a median value (over countries and sectors) of 12, with higher median ratios for two countries that enjoy preferential access to the U.S. market, Peru (48 times larger) and Colombia (24 times larger).

---

[60] Previous simulations are mainly based on the sample excluding the United States. In this exercise we use the estimations based on the sample including this country.

Figure 3.12. Reductions in Transport Costs and Tariffs and Median Response of Sectoral Exports to the U.S.

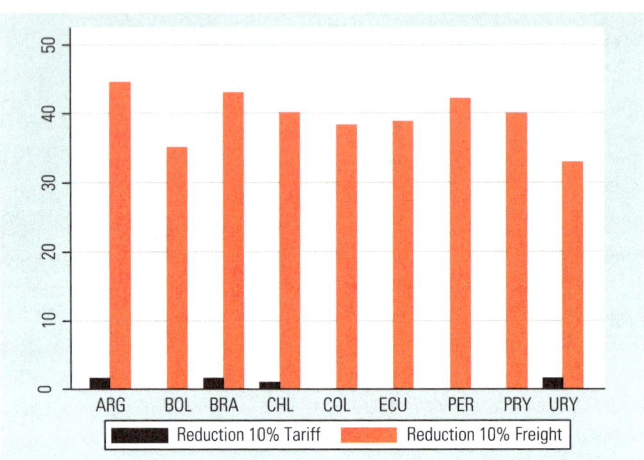

The figure shows the median predicted percentage change of exports to the United States across sectors as a consequence of a 10 percent reduction in transport costs and a 10 percent reduction in tariffs for selected Latin American countries, as computed using estimation results from the specification including importer, exporter, and year fixed effect and including the United States, and taking 2004 as a benchmark. Exporter countries are on the horizontal axis.

Summing Up

This section has examined how trade costs affect trade in nine Latin American countries. Our findings suggest that these costs are important impediments for both import and export volumes as well as for import and export diversification. Thus, a 10 percent decrease in trade costs would increase imports by 50 percent, intraregional exports more than 60 percent, the number of imported products by 9 percent, and that of intraregional exported products by more than 10 percent.

The trade-increasing effect of declines in transport costs would be larger than that of tariffs. More precisely, a given reduction in transport costs is expected to lead to a median expansion of intraregional exports almost 5 times larger and to a median increase in the number of products exported to the region 3 times larger than a similar reduction in tariffs. Depending on the country and the sector, this increase may be several times larger. The highest median ratio of effects on export volumes would

Figure 3.13. Reductions in Transport Costs and Tariffs and Response of Export Diversification in the U.S.

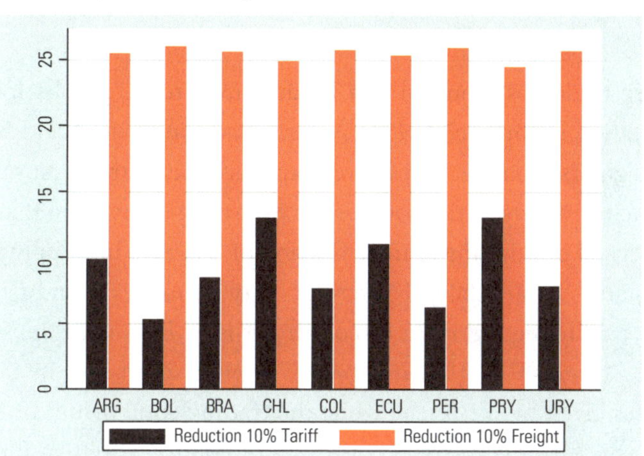

The figure shows the predicted percentage change in the number of products exported to the United States as a consequence of a 10 percent reduction in transport costs and a 10 percent reduction in tariffs for selected Latin American countries, as computed using estimation results from the specification including importer, exporter, and year fixed effect and including the United States, and taking 2004 as a benchmark. Exporter countries are on the horizontal axis.

be observed in Brazil (6.1 times larger) and Ecuador (6.0 times larger) and in the fertilizers sector (6.1 times larger), while that on export diversification would correspond to Uruguay (4.4 times larger) and Peru (3.6 times larger). Similar patterns might be expected in exports to the United States. In Chapter 2 we have seen that, on average, transport costs in Latin America would decline by 20 percent if countries in the region had the U.S. port efficiency level. The estimates we report in this chapter suggest that this would have a substantial impact on LAC's export performance.

The previous results reflect the contrast between the advances made on intraregional tariff liberalization and the delay in addressing trade-related infrastructure gaps. The policy implications are clear. A more balanced trade agenda should include the improvements in all aspects of the region's infrastructure, with a clear aim to bring transport costs closer to levels observed in the developed world. Without significant improvements in this area, an expanded and more diversified LAC presence in the world markets will remain an elusive goal.

Appendix 3.A
Iceberg Trade Cost

The iceberg trade cost concept can be described using graphs following the presentation in Mundell (1957). Assume two countries, *A* and *B*, which export two goods, *X* and *Z*, respectively, and assume further that transport costs are incurred only in the good of the exporting country, so that a fraction of *X* is used in shipping *X* and a fraction of *Z* is used in shipping *Z*. The curves O_{A1} and O_{B1} are the CIF offer curves of countries *A* and *B*, respectively. The trading equilibrium of country *A* is at E_A, where this country exports LE_A of good *X* in return for *HP* of good *Z*, so that its domestic price ratio is given by the line *a*, while the trading equilibrium of country *B* is at E_B, where this country exports HE_B of good *Z* in return for *OH* of good *X*, so that its domestic price ratio is given by the line *b*. Country *A* exports LE_A of good *X*, but country *B* only receives *LP*, since PE_A is used up in transporting *X*. Similarly, country *B* exports HE_B of good *Z*, but country *A* only receives *LP*, since PE_B is used up in transporting *Z*. The difference between the exports of one country and the imports of the other country is consumed in transport costs.

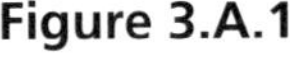
Figure 3.A.1

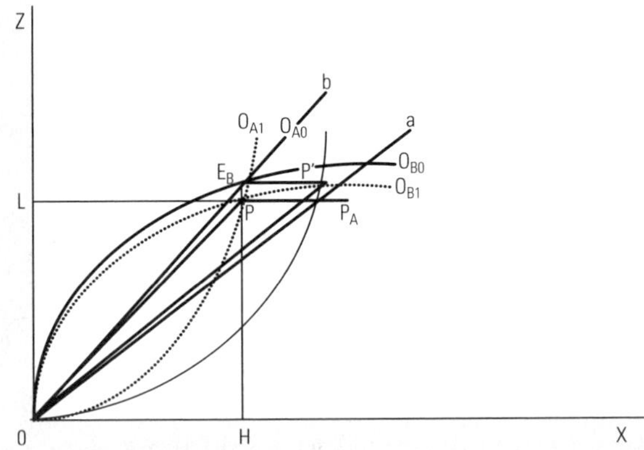

Appendix 3.B
Dataset

Table 3.B.1. Country Coverage

1995	2000	2001	2002	2003	2004	2005
Colombia	Argentina	Argentina	Argentina	Argentina	Argentina	Argentina
Peru	Brazil	Brazil	Bolivia	Brazil	Bolivia	Brazil
Uruguay	Chile	Chile	Brazil	Chile	Brazil	Chile
	Colombia	Peru	Chile	Ecuador	Chile	Peru
	Peru	Paraguay	Peru	Peru	Ecuador	Uruguay
	Paraguay	Uruguay	Paraguay	Uruguay	Peru	United States
	Uruguay	United States	Uruguay	United States	Uruguay	
	United States		United States		United States	

Appendix 3.C
Empirical Methodology

This appendix derives the estimation equation using insights from both the multi-sector model developed by Hummels (2001) and that proposed by Hallak (2006) and discusses the main econometric issues.

Consider a world composed of C countries indexed by $c = 1, \ldots, C$. In each country there is a representative consumer with a two-tier utility function. The upper-tier utility is weakly separable into sub-utility indexes defined for each sector $i = 1, \ldots, I$:

$$U_c = U\left[u_{c1}, \ldots, u_{cI}\right] \quad \text{(C.1)}$$

The sub-utility index is a general function of the quantity consumed of the good q that takes the following form:

$$u_{ck} = \left[\sum_{d \in C} \sum_{z \in Z_k} \left(\theta_{cdk} q_{cdz}\right)^{\frac{\sigma_k - 1}{\sigma_k}}\right]^{\frac{\sigma_k}{\sigma_k - 1}} \quad \text{(C.2)}$$

where u_{ck} is defined over all varieties $z \in Z_k$ in sector k, θ_{cdk} is a preference parameter for (country-) specific varieties within sector k, and σ_k is the elasticity of substitution in sector k.

Consumers in country c face a price p_{cdz} for variety z from country d. This price is given by $p_{cdz} = p_{dk}\tau_{cdz} + \tilde{f}_{cdz}$, where we assume that all varieties z produced by country d in sector k are symmetric; $\tau_{cdz} = 1 + (T_{cdz}/M_{cdz}) = 1 + \rho_{cdz}$ is the real tariff rate applied by country c on good z originated in country d and T_{cdz} is the actual tariff revenue on this good; and $\tilde{f}_{cdz} = F_{cdz}/q_{cdz}$ is the per unit shipping charge and F_{cdz} is total transportation expenditures (freight plus insurance) on good z from country d.

The consumer uses two-stage budgeting. In the first stage, for a given allocation across sectors $E_{c1}, \ldots, E_{cI}$, expenditure in variety z in sector k from country d is given by:

$$M_{cdz} = p_{dk}q_{cdz} = \theta_{cdk}^{\sigma_k - 1} \frac{p_{dk}^{1-\sigma_k}\left(\tau_{cdz} + f_{cdz}\right)^{1-\sigma_k}}{\sum_{d\in C}\sum_{z\in Z_k} \theta_{cdk}^{\sigma_k-1} p_{dk}^{1-\sigma_k}\left(\tau_{cdz} + f_{cdz}\right)^{1-\sigma_k}} E_{ck} \quad \text{(C.3)}$$

where M_{cdz} is country c's total imports of variety z in sector k from country d and $f_{cdz} = F_{cdz}/M_{cdz}$ (so $f_{cdz} = \tilde{f}_{cdz}/p_{cdz}$) is the ad valorem transport cost for good z from country d to country c.[61]

Taking natural logarithms in Equation (C.3), we get:

$$\begin{aligned} lnM_{cdk} &= (\sigma_k - 1)ln\,\theta_{cdk} + (1-\sigma_k)lnp_{dk} \\ &\quad -(1-\sigma_k)ln(\tau_{cdz} + f_{cdz}) + lnP_{ck} + lnE_{ck} \end{aligned} \quad \text{(C.4)}$$

where P_{ci} is the price index for importer c in sector k.

We assume that the preference parameter is captured through observable proxies (see Hummels 2001) plus a random component (see, e.g., Combes, Lafourcade and Mayer 2005). In particular, consumers are

[61] Assuming common trade costs across varieties and aggregating at the sectoral level, one gets:

$$M_{cdk} = n_{dk}\theta_{cdk}^{\sigma_k-1} \frac{p_{dk}^{1-\sigma_k}\left(\tau_{cdk} + f_{cdk}\right)^{1-\sigma_k}}{\sum_{d\in C}\sum_{z\in Z_k} p_{dk}^{1-\sigma_k}\left(\tau_{cdz} + f_{cdz}\right)^{1-\sigma_k}} E_{ck}$$

where n_{dk} is the number of varieties in sector k in country d. Closing this model requires solving for the number of varieties in each sector. In this case, the sectoral level of trade depends on trade barriers directly, through substitution, and indirectly, through the effect on production, which magnifies the former (see Hummels 2001).

assumed to have systematic preferences for varieties on which they have more information and this is assumed to be specifically the case for those varieties originating in closer countries (see Combes et al. 2005).[62] Formally, $(\sigma_k - 1) ln\,\theta_{cdk} = \delta_k lnD_{cd} + \varepsilon_{cdk}$, where D is the bilateral distance between country c and country d and ε is an error term.[63] The second term on the right-hand side of Equation (C.4) takes the same value for all importers and hence will be absorbed into exporter-specific fixed effects, i.e., $\lambda_{dk} = (1-\sigma_k) lnp_{dk}$. Similarly, the fourth and fifth terms on the right-hand side take the same value when country c is the importer, regardless of the identity of the exporter, so that will be accounted for by importer-specific fixed effects, that is, $\lambda_{ck} = \ln P_{ck} + \ln E_{ck}$. These fixed effects also allow us to control for all unobserved time invariant factors that are not specific to the bilateral pair, such as non-tariff barriers that are common to all partners and systematic differences across reporters in their freight charge valuation methods, thus reducing the scope for omitted variables and mis-measurement (see Hummels 2001). The estimation equation therefore becomes:

$$lnM_{cdz} = \lambda_{ck} + \lambda_{dk} + \beta_k ln(\tau_{cdz} + f_{cdz}) + \delta_k \ln D_{cd} + \varepsilon_{cdk} \qquad \text{(C.5)}$$

where the coefficient on the natural logarithm of freight plus tariffs allows calculating the CES elasticity for that good ($\beta_k = 1-\sigma_k$). This is the case because the data includes prices in the form of tariff and freight rates and the bilateral variation in these explicit trade costs plus exporter fixed effects exactly identifies the variation in prices faced by importers (see Hummels 2001).[64]

---

[62] Distance can be considered a proxy for informational costs (see, e.g., Grossman 1998; Anderson 2000; Portes, Rey and Oh 2001; Loungani, Mody and Razin 2002; Guiso, Sapienza and Zingales 2005; Combes, Lafourcade and Mayer 2005; and Hwang 2007).

[63] In one of our robustness exercises, we control for the influence of additional variables by assuming that $(\sigma_k - 1) ln\,\theta_{cdk} = \delta_k lnD_{cd} + \theta_k B_{cd} + \gamma_k L_{cd} + \varepsilon_{cdk}$, where B is a binary variable informing whether trading partners share a border and L is a binary variable indicating whether their populations share a language. We specifically assume that preference is stronger for varieties coming from neighbor countries and from those countries with the same language as this may proxy similar cultural backgrounds. Accordingly, the expected effect of these variables on trade is positive.

[64] Freight and tariffs would be insufficient for identification if firms price to market because in this case trade costs affect prices exclusive of these costs.

When estimating Equation (C.5), individual observations, which are total imports into country *c* from country *d* in a six-digit HS variety, are pooled at the sectoral level as defined by the two-digit HS classification. In other words, we estimate one equation for each good pooling over the corresponding varieties. In doing this, we assume that the impact of trade costs and other relevant variables is identical across varieties.

As a starting point, we estimate a fully pooled version of Equation (C.5) over all goods, that is,

$$lnM_{cdz} = \lambda_c + \lambda_d + \lambda_k + \beta ln\left(\tau_{cdz} + f_{cdz}\right) + \delta \ln D_{cd} + \varepsilon_{cdk} \qquad \text{(C.6)}$$

This equation provides us with a measure of the average effect of these costs on imports across sectors over all products.[65] Equations (C.5) and (C.6) are estimated by OLS. Operatively, estimating Equation (C.5), especially for imports, implies a priori a formidable, almost unfeasible task. Our full database has approximately 2,500,000 observations over seven years. Reporting countries potentially import more than 5,000 products from more than 200 partners. Thus, we have up to four sets of fixed effects two of which, product and partner, are extremely large. To estimate this four-way error component model, we include the smaller sets of effects as dummy variables (i.e., country and year) and sweep out the larger ones by the within transformation, applying the decomposition of the design matrix proposed by Cornelissen (2006).[66]

---

[65] The main drawback of this exercise is that resorting to cross-commodity variation to estimate the effects of trade costs can be seen as estimating a demand equation by comparing demand of different goods and thus can be potentially problematic (see Leamer 1990). This problem is mitigated in our estimations at the sectoral level.

[66] If the number of groups is high, the design matrix including the dummy variables may become prohibitively large for computer packages. Cornelissen (2006) proposes a decomposition of this matrix consisting of creating the cross-product matrices for the least square normal equations without explicitly creating the dummy variables for the group effects. Since the cross-product matrices are of much lower dimension than the design matrix, this procedure reduces the computer memory required considerably.

Appendix 3.D
Estimation Results

Table 3.D.1. Trade Costs, Imports, and Exports

	Imports				Exports			
	All Countries		Excluding U.S.		All Countries		Excluding U.S.	
Variables								
Freight and Tariffs	−5.240***	−5.790***	−4.818***	−5.416***	−5.188***	−5.860***	−6.131***	−6.975***
	(0.014)	(0.014)	(0.015)	(0.016)	(0.027)	(0.028)	(0.035)	(0.036)
Distance	−0.591***	−0.572***	−0.271***	−0.256***	−0.339***	−0.315***	−0.183***	−0.143***
	(0.004)	(0.004)	(0.007)	(0.007)	(0.007)	(0.007)	(0.008)	(0.009)
Country Fixed Effects	Yes	No	Yes	No	Yes	No	Yes	No
Partner Fixed Effects	Yes	No	Yes	No	Yes	No	Yes	No
Country-Year Fixed Effects	No	Yes	No	Yes	No	Yes	No	Yes
Partner-Year Fixed Effects	No	Yes	No	Yes	No	Yes	No	Yes
Year Fixed Effects	Yes	Yes	Yes	Yes	Yes	Yes	Yes	Yes

The table presents OLS estimations of Equation (C.6) using import, freight and insurance, and tariff data for Argentina, Bolivia, Brazil, Chile, Colombia, Ecuador, Paraguay, Peru, the United States, and Uruguay for the periods 1995 and 2000–2005. Freight and tariffs is defined as the natural logarithm of one plus actually collected tariff revenues divided by imports plus freight (and insurance) divided by imports. Distance is the natural logarithm of the geodesic distance between pairs of cities as calculated using the great-circle formula (see CEPII). Observations for which transport costs plus tariffs exceed the amount traded are dropped. Standard errors are in parentheses below the estimated coefficients.

* significant at 10%; ** significant at 5%; and *** significant at 1%.

Table 3.D.2. Trade Costs, Imports, and Exports—Robustness: Sample

	Imports				Exports			
	All Countries		Excluding U.S.		All Countries		Excluding U.S.	
Variables								
Freight and Tariffs	−5.416***	−4.818***	−5.790***	−5.240***	−5.364***	−4.800***	−5.416***	−5.395***
	(0.016)	(0.015)	(0.014)	(0.014)	(0.016)	(0.016)	(0.016)	(0.016)
Distance	−0.256***	−0.271***	−0.572***	−0.591***	−0.214***	−0.229***	−0.256***	−0.249***
	(0.007)	(0.007)	(0.004)	(0.004)	(0.007)	(0.007)	(0.007)	(0.007)
Country Fixed Effects	Yes	No	Yes	No	Yes	No	Yes	No
Partner Fixed Effects	Yes	No	Yes	No	Yes	No	Yes	No
Country-Year Fixed Effects	No	Yes	No	Yes	No	Yes	No	Yes
Partner-Year Fixed Effects	No	Yes	No	Yes	No	Yes	No	Yes
Year Fixed Effects	Yes	Yes	Yes	Yes	Yes	Yes	Yes	Yes

The table presents OLS estimations of Equation (C.6) using import, freight and insurance, and tariff data for Argentina, Bolivia, Brazil, Chile, Colombia, Ecuador, Paraguay, Peru, the United States, and Uruguay for the periods 1995 and 2000-2005. Freight and tariffs is defined as the natural logarithm of one plus actually collected tariff revenues divided by imports plus freight (and insurance) divided by imports. Distance is the natural logarithm of the geodesic distance between pairs of cities as calculated using the great-circle formula (see CEPII). Observations for which transport costs or tariffs individually exceed the amount traded are dropped. Standard errors are in parentheses below the estimated coefficients.

* significant at 10%; ** significant at 5%; and *** significant at 1%.[67]

[67] Similar results, although smaller in magnitude, are found when trade flows smaller than US$5,000 are excluded.

Table 3.D.3. Trade Costs, Imports, and Exports—Robustness: Other Gravity Variables

Variables	Imports				Exports			
	All Countries		Excluding U.S.		All Countries		Excluding U.S.	
Freight and Tariffs	−5.768***	−5.217***	−5.429***	−4.827***	−5.780***	−5.862***	−6.812***	−6.863***
	(0.015)	(0.014)	(0.016)	(0.015)	(0.033)	(0.043)	(0.035)	(0.045)
Distance	−0.464***	−0.470***	−0.221***	−0.226***	−0.381***	−0.166***	−0.357***	−0.230***
	(0.005)	(0.005)	(0.008)	(0.007)	(0.009)	(0.012)	(0.009)	(0.010)
Common Border	0.296***	0.335***	0.052***	0.096***	0.045***	0.063***	0.094***	0.028**
	(0.010)	(0.010)	(0.012)	(0.012)	(0.013)	(0.015)	(0.013)	(0.014)
Common Language	0.096***	0.099***	0.172***	0.173***				
	(0.007)	(0.007)	(0.011)	(0.011)				
Country Fixed Effects	Yes	No	Yes	No	Yes	No	Yes	No
Partner Fixed Effects	Yes	No	Yes	No	Yes	No	Yes	No
Country-Year Fixed Effects	No	Yes	No	Yes	No	Yes	No	Yes
Partner-Year Fixed Effects	No	Yes	No	Yes	No	Yes	No	Yes
Year Fixed Effects	Yes	Yes	Yes	Yes	Yes	Yes	Yes	Yes

The table presents OLS estimations of Equation (C.6) using import, freight and insurance, and tariff data for Argentina, Bolivia, Brazil, Chile, Colombia, Ecuador, Paraguay, Peru, the United States, and Uruguay for the periods 1995 and 2000–2005. Freight and tariffs is defined as the natural logarithm of one plus actually collected tariff revenues divided by imports plus freight (and insurance) divided by imports. Distance is the natural logarithm of the geodesic distance between pairs of cities as calculated using the great-circle formula (see CEPII). Common border (common language) is a binary variable taking the value of one if the importer and the exporter countries share a border (at least 9% of the population of the importer and the exporter countries speak the same language) and zero otherwise. Observations for which transport costs plus tariffs exceed the amount traded are dropped. Standard errors are in parentheses below the estimated coefficients.

* significant at 10%; ** significant at 5%; and *** significant at 1%.

Table 3.D.4. Trade Costs, Imports, and Exports—Year-by-Year Estimations

	Imports				Exports			
	All Countries		Excluding U.S.		All Countries		Excluding U.S.	
Year	F and T	D	F and T	D	F and T	D	F and T	D
2000	−5.740***	−0.584***	−5.391***	−0.287***	−6.050***	−0.204**	−7.521***	−0.0301**
	(0.037)	(0.010)	(0.041)	(0.018)	(0.240)	(0.088)	(0.380)	(0.015)
2001	−5.711***	−0.611***	−5.314***	−0.323***	−6.096***	−0.222***	−7.567***	−0.078**
	(0.037)	(0.011)	(0.041)	(0.020)	(0.240)	(0.068)	(0.390)	(0.037)
2002	−5.312***	−0.617***	−4.913***	−0.304***	−5.468***	−0.246***	−6.226***	−0.134**
	(0.034)	(0.010)	(0.037)	(0.018)	(0.150)	(0.055)	(0.150)	(0.057)
2003	−6.118***	−0.559***	−5.822***	−0.247***	−6.393***	−0.226***	−7.686***	−0.110**
	(0.036)	(0.010)	(0.040)	(0.015)	(0.360)	(0.040)	(0.550)	(0.036)
2004	−5.926***	−0.562***	−5.627***	−0.208***	−6.477***	−0.239***	−7.697***	−0.153**
	(0.034)	(0.009)	(0.037)	(0.015)	(0.470)	(0.041)	(0.570)	(0.050)
2005	−6.395***	−0.565***	−5.992***	−0.231***	−6.332***	−0.204**	−7.689***	−0.148**
	(0.038)	(0.010)	(0.043)	(0.020)	(0.500)	(0.063)	(0.570)	(0.053)
Country Fixed Effects	Yes	Yes	Yes	Yes	Yes	Yes	Yes	Yes
Partner Fixed Effects	Yes	Yes	Yes	Yes	Yes	Yes	Yes	Yes

The table presents year-by-year OLS estimations of Equation (C.6) using import, freight and insurance, and tariff data for Argentina, Bolivia, Brazil, Chile, Colombia, Ecuador, Paraguay, Peru, the United States, and Uruguay for the period 2000–2005. Freight and tariffs is defined as the natural logarithm of one plus actually collected tariff revenues divided by imports plus freight (and insurance) divided by imports. Distance is the natural logarithm of the geodesic distance between pairs of cities as calculated using the great-circle formula (see CEPII). Observations for which transport costs plus tariffs exceed the amount traded are dropped. Standard errors are in parentheses below the estimated coefficients.

* significant at 10%; ** significant at 5%; and *** significant at 1%.

Table 3.D.5. Trade Costs and Trade Diversification

	Imports				Exports			
Variables	**All Countries**		**Excluding U.S.**		**All Countries**		**Excluding U.S.**	
Freight and Tariffs	−1.498***	−1.640***	−0.897***	−0.712***	−2.254***	−3.497***	−1.278**	−2.182*
	(0.210)	(0.260)	(0.200)	(0.250)	(0.840)	(1.080)	(0.561)	(1.250)
Distance	−0.578***	−0.547***	−0.851***	−0.851***	−0.912***	−0.862***	−0.988***	−0.929***
	(0.038)	(0.040)	(0.047)	(0.049)	(0.049)	(0.056)	(0.047)	(0.068)
Country Fixed Effects	Yes	No	Yes	No	Yes	No	Yes	No
Partner Fixed Effects	Yes	No	Yes	No	Yes	No	Yes	No
Country-Year Fixed Effects	No	Yes	No	Yes	No	Yes	No	Yes
Partner-Year Fixed Effects	No	Yes	No	Yes	No	Yes	No	Yes
Year Fixed Effects	Yes	Yes	Yes	Yes	Yes	Yes	Yes	Yes

The table presents year-by-year OLS estimations of Equation (C.7) using import, freight and insurance, and tariff data for Argentina, Bolivia, Brazil, Chile, Colombia, Ecuador, Paraguay, Peru, the United States, and Uruguay for the periods 1995 and 2000–2005. Freight and tariffs is defined as the natural logarithm of one plus the simple average across products of actually collected tariff revenues plus freight (and insurance) divided by imports. Distance is the natural logarithm of the geodesic distance between pairs of cities as calculated using the great-circle formula (see CEPII). Observations for which transport costs plus tariffs exceed the amount traded are dropped. Standard errors are in parentheses below the estimated coefficients.

* significant at 10%; ** significant at 5%; and *** significant at 1%.

Table 3.D.6. Trade Costs and Trade Diversification—Robustness: Other Trade Cost Measures

	Imports				Exports			
Variables	All Countries		Excluding U.S.		All Countries		Excluding U.S.	
Freight and Tariffs	−0.860**	−0.826**	−0.124**	−0.121**	−1.485*	−1.917*	−0.891***	−1.449***
	(0.344)	(0.315)	(0.059)	(0.057)	(0.690)	(0.890)	(0.740)	(1.140)
Distance	−0.576***	−0.552***	−0.651***	−0.630***	−0.878***	−0.852***	−0.957***	−0.917***
	(0.160)	(0.154)	(0.149)	(0.218)	(0.170)	(0.190)	(0.160)	(0.190)
Country Fixed Effects	Yes	No	Yes	No	Yes	No	Yes	No
Partner Fixed Effects	Yes	No	Yes	No	Yes	No	Yes	No
Country-Year Fixed Effects	No	Yes	No	Yes	No	Yes	No	Yes
Partner-Year Fixed Effects	No	Yes	No	Yes	No	Yes	No	Yes
Year Fixed Effects	Yes	Yes	Yes	Yes	Yes	Yes	Yes	Yes

The table presents year-by-year OLS estimations of Equation (C.7) using import, freight and insurance, and tariff data for Argentina, Bolivia, Brazil, Chile, Colombia, Ecuador, Paraguay, Peru, the United States, and Uruguay for the periods 1995 and 2000–2005. Freight and tariffs is defined as the natural logarithm of one plus total bilateral freight plus insurance divided by total bilateral imports, plus actually collected tariff revenues divided by bilateral imports. Distance is the natural logarithm of the geodesic distance between pairs of cities as calculated using the great-circle formula (see CEPII). Observations for which transport costs plus tariffs exceed the amount traded are dropped. Standard errors are in parentheses below the estimated coefficients.

* significant at 10%; ** significant at 5%; and *** significant at 1%.

Table 3.D.7. Trade Costs and Trade Diversification—Robustness: Other Gravity Variables

	Imports				Exports			
Variables	**All Countries**		**Excluding U.S.**		**All Countries**		**Excluding U.S.**	
Freight and Tariffs	−1.406***	−1.525***	−0.876***	−0.716***	−1.839**	−2.943***	−0.989**	−1.775***
	(0.210)	(0.260)	(0.200)	(0.250)	(0.800)	(1.040)	(0.410)	(0.860)
Distance	−0.454***	−0.419***	−0.731***	−0.725***	−0.716***	−0.683***	−0.754***	−0.705***
	(0.042)	(0.044)	(0.051)	(0.054)	(0.056)	(0.063)	(0.070)	(0.079)
Common Border	0.474***	0.478***	0.292***	0.277***	0.488***	0.461***	0.488***	0.473***
	(0.086)	(0.091)	(0.086)	(0.087)	(0.078)	(0.085)	(0.088)	(0.098)
Common Language	0.470***	0.469***	0.453***	0.482***				
	(0.045)	(0.047)	(0.067)	(0.068)				
Country Fixed Effects	Yes	No	Yes	No	Yes	No	Yes	No
Partner Fixed Effects	Yes	No	Yes	No	Yes	No	Yes	No
Country-Year Fixed Effects	No	Yes	No	Yes	No	Yes	No	Yes
Partner-Year Fixed Effects	No	Yes	No	Yes	No	Yes	No	Yes
Year Fixed Effects	Yes	Yes	Yes	Yes	Yes	Yes	Yes	Yes

The table presents year-by-year OLS estimations of Equation (C.7) using import, freight and insurance, and tariff data for Argentina, Bolivia, Brazil, Chile, Colombia, Ecuador, Paraguay, Peru, the United States, and Uruguay for the periods 1995 and 2000–2005. Freight and tariffs is defined as the natural logarithm of one plus the simple average across products of actually collected tariff revenues plus freight (and insurance) divided by imports. Distance is the natural logarithm of the geodesic distance between pairs of cities as calculated using the great-circle formula (see CEPII). Observations for which transport costs plus tariffs exceed the amount traded are dropped. Standard errors are in parentheses below the estimated coefficients.

* significant at 10%; ** significant at 5%; and *** significant at 1%.

References

Anderson, J. 2000. Why Do Countries Trade (So Little)? *Pacific Economic Review* 5: 115–134.

Anderson, J., and E. van Wincoop. 2004. Trade Costs. *Journal of Economic Literature* 42(3): 691–751.

Baier, S., and J. Bergstrand. 2001. The Growth of World Trade: Tariffs, Transport Costs, and Income Similarity. *Journal of International Economics* 53(1): 1–27.

Balassa, B. 1961. *The Theory of Economic Integration*. Homewood, IL: Richard Irwin, Inc.

Baldwin, R., and D. Taglioni. 2006. *Gravity for Dummies and Dummies for Gravity Equations*. Working Paper 12516. Cambridge, MA: National Bureau of Economic Research.

Baltagi, B. 1995. *Econometric Analysis of Panel Data*. New York: John Wiley and Sons.

Beckerman, W. 1956. Distance and the Patterns of Intra-European Trade. *Review of Economics and Statistics* 38(1) 31–40.

Broda, C., and D. Weinstein. 2006. Globalization and the Gains from Variety. *Quarterly Journal of Economics* 121(2): 541–585.

Bun, M., and F. Klaassen. 2002. *The Importance of Dynamics in Panel Gravity Models of Trade*. Discussion Paper 2002/18, University of Amsterdam.

Cadot, O., C. Carrere and V. Strauss-Kahn. 2007. Export Diversification: What Is Behind the Hump? Washington, D.C.: Inter-American Development Bank, mimeo.

Calderón, C., and L. Servén. 2004. *Trends in Infrastructure in Latin America, 1980–2001*. Working Paper 169. Banco Central de Chile.

Clark, X., D. Dollar and A. Micco. 2004. Port Efficiency, Maritime Transport Costs, and Bilateral Trade. *Journal of Development Economics* 75(2): 417–450.

Cleveland, W. 1979. Robust Locally Weighted Regression and Smoothing Scatterplots. *Journal of the American Statistical Association* 74(368): 829–836.

Combes, P., M. Lafourcade and T. Mayer. 2005. The Trade-Creating Effects of Business and Social Networks: Evidence from France. *Journal of International Economics* 66(1): 1–29.

Cornelissen, T. 2006. *Using STATA for a Memory Saving Fixed-Effects Estimation of the Three-Way Error Component Model.* FDZ Methodenreport 3/2006. Bundesagentur fuer Arbeit.

De, P. 2006. *Why Trade Costs Matter?* Working Paper 7. Asia-Pacific Research and Training Network on Trade.

Falvey, R. 1976. Transport Costs in the Pure Theory of International Trade. *Economic Journal* 86(343): 536–550.

Geraci, V., and W. Prewo. 1977. Bilateral Trade Flows and Transport Costs. *Review of Economics and Statistics* 59(1): 67–74.

Goodall, C. 1990. A Survey of Smoothing Techniques. In *Modern Methods of Data Analysis*, ed. J. Fox and J. Long. Newbury Park, CA: Sage Publications.

Greene, W. 1997. *Econometric Analysis.* Upper Saddle River, NJ: Prentice Hall.

Grossman, G. 1998. Comments on Alan V. Deardorff, *Determinants of Bilateral Trade: Does Gravity Work in a Neoclassical World?* In *The Regionalization of the World Economy*, ed. J. Frankel. Chicago: University of Chicago, for National Bureau of Economic Research (NBER).

Guiso, L., P. Sapienza and L. Zingales. 2005. Cultural Biases in Economic Exchange. University of Chicago, mimeo.

Hallak, J. 2006. Product Quality and the Direction of Trade. *Journal of International Economics* 68(1) 238–265.

Harrigan, J. 1993. OECD Imports and Trade Barriers in 1983. *Journal of International Economics* 34(1–2): 91–111.

Helpman, E., M. Melitz and Y. Rubinstein. 2007. *Estimating Trade Flows: Trading Partners and Trading Volumes.* Working Paper 12927. Cambridge, MA: National Bureau of Economic Research.

Hummels, D. 2001. Towards a Geography of Trade Costs. West Lafayette, IN: Purdue University, mimeo.

Hummels, D., and A. Skiba. 2004a. Shipping the Good Apples Out? An Empirical Confirmation of the Alchian-Allen Conjecture. *Journal of Political Economy* 112(6): 1384–1402.

Hummels, D., and A. Skiba. 2004b. A Virtuous Cycle? Regional Tariff Liberalization and Scale Economies in Transport. In *FTAA and Beyond: Prospects for Integration in the Americas,* ed. A. Estevadeordal, D. Rodrik, A. M. Taylor and A. Velasco. Cambridge, MA: Harvard University Press.

Hummels, D., and V. Lugovskyy. 2006. Are Matched Partner Trade Statistics a Usable Measure of Transportation Costs? *Review of International Economics* 14(1): 69–86.

Hummels, D., V. Lugovskyy and A. Skiba. 2007. The Trade Reducing Effects of Market Power in International Shipping. Working Paper 12914. Cambridge, MA: National Bureau of Economic Research.

Hwang, R. 2007. Distance and Trade: Disentangling Unfamiliarity Effects and Transport Cost Effects. *European Economic Review* 51(1): 161–181.

Imbs, J., and R. Wacziarg. 2003. Stages of Diversification. *American Economic Review* 93(1): 63–86.

Krugman, P. 1980. Scale Economies, Product Differentiation, and the Pattern of Trade. *American Economic Review* 70(5): 950–959.

Krugman, P. 1991. Increasing Returns and Economic Geography. *Journal of Political Economy* 99(3): 483–499.

Leamer, E. 1990. Latin America as a Target of Trade Barriers Erected by the Major Developed Countries in 1983. *Journal of Development Economics* 32(2): 337–368.

Limao, N., and A. Venables. 2001. Infrastructure, Geographical Disadvantage, Transport Costs and Trade. *World Bank Economic Review* 15(3): 451–479.

Loungani, P., A. Mody and A. Razin. 2002. The Global Disconnect: The Role of Transactional Distance and Scale Economies in the Gravity Equation. *Scottish Journal of Political Economy* 49(5): 526–543.

Martínez-Zarzoso, I., and C. Suárez-Burguet. 2005. Transport Costs and Trade: Empirical Evidence for Latin American Imports from the

European Union. *Journal of International Trade and Economic Development* 14(3): 353–371.

Mundell, R. 1957. Transport Costs in International Trade Theory. *Canadian Journal of Economics and Political Science* 23(3): 331–348.

Portes, R., H. Rey and Y. Oh. 2001. Information and Capital Flows: The Determinants of Transactions in Financial Assets. *European Economic Review* 45(4-6): 783–796.

Roberts, M., and J. Tybout. 1997. The Decision to Export in Colombia: An Empirical Model of Entry with Sunk Costs. *American Economic Review* 87(4): 545–564.

Ruiz, J., and J. Vilarrubia. 2007. *The Wise Use of Dummies in Gravity Models: Export Potentials in the EUROMED Region*. Working Paper 720. Banco de España.

Samuelson, P. 1954. The Transfer Problem and Transport Costs: Analysis of Effects of Trade Impediments. *Economic Journal* 64(254): 264–289.

Silverman, B. 1986. *Density Estimation for Statistics and Data Analysis.* New York: Chapman and Hall.

World Bank. Various years. *World Development Indicators.* Washington, D.C.: World Bank.

CHAPTER 4

The Reality on the Ground: Case Studies of Ecuador, Brazil, Argentina and Mexico

This report has so far been mainly about statistical significance. We have tried to use the best data and models available to show that nowadays transport costs have surpassed tariff and non-tariff barriers to become the major obstacle to the region's trade, except for a few well-known exceptions, particularly in agriculture. Even though this is the scientific approach when one is trying to settle what is essentially an empirical argument, relying just on fairly aggregated data and regressions might have the unwanted side effect of alienating the reader, particularly the non-technical reader, who may fail to see the connection between an abstract, quantitative analysis and the so-called real issues on the ground.

To protect ourselves against this side effect, in this chapter we report on four country studies—Ecuador, Brazil, Argentina and Mexico—which try to illustrate at the product level what the issues discussed so far mean for people in the region trying to trade goods across borders. As with case studies in general, ours suffer from what economists call a selection bias. That is, the cases were not selected randomly. Rather, the selection reflected a combination of demand (i.e. our intent to illustrate the role of transport costs in the trade of both natural resources and manufactured goods) and supply (the availability of specialists and data on a particular time, country and product) factors.

Our main concern here, though, is not with statistical significance, but with providing the reader with an opportunity to see, in very concrete, everyday-life terms, how transport costs interact with countries' comparative advantages to block or provide opportunities to trade. The case studies themselves are not intended as formal statistical exercises, but as an eclectic attempt to tell a realistic story about the impact of transport costs on trade, using information ranging from interviews with representatives of firms and sector associations to more traditional trade data. We will focus on their more significant findings, leaving the reader the option of consulting the background papers of this report (see references) for the full version of these studies.

Ecuador: A Time-Sensitive Story about Cut Flowers[68]

Cut flowers are perhaps one of the best examples of how transport costs and comparative advantages interact to generate valuable export opportunities for LAC. Cut flowers fit perfectly with the definition of time-sensitive goods discussed in Chapter 1. According to industry estimates, roses, for instance, can last up to 14 days after harvesting if handled properly. Assuming a modest retail shelf life expectancy of seven days, any shipping time that goes beyond seven days (including both domestic and international transportation) imposes a heavy depreciation cost to traders. So, proximity is definitely an advantage. Beyond being time sensitive, cut flowers are also labor intensive, given that the harvest cannot be fully mechanized, and natural resource intensive, since the quality and availability of land, as well as the characteristics of the climate, are key factors for the success of the industry.

These characteristics, coupled with recent development in air transportation and refrigeration, have opened opportunities for trade, particularly for North-South trade, in a fast growing world market whose size is estimated between US$40 and US$60 billion annually, 80 percent of which is concentrated in the United States (15 percent) and the EU (65 percent). The search for land and cheaper labor to cater for this large and growing demand has been forcing production to move south to developing countries in Asia, Africa and in LAC. As proximity would indicate, the U.S. market has been the focus of the region's exports. In 2005, approximately 82 percent of U.S. imports of cut flowers originated in the Western

[68] This section was adapted from Vega (2008).

Hemisphere, with Colombia and Ecuador accounting, respectively, for 59 and 18 percent of the total.

The story of Ecuador's success in this industry is marked, on the one hand, by a perfect match between product characteristics and the country's factor endowments, and on the other, by a constant effort to overcome the difficulties created by the country's precarious infrastructure. The climate (an altitude higher than 2,000 meters above sea level in the equatorial zone), the availability of rich volcanic soils, low labor costs and the relative proximity to the United States served as a perfect platform for floriculture to develop. Yet, the shortcomings of Ecuador's infrastructure, as well as the failures to acquire the necessary expertise, meant that the development of the industry was a lengthy and tortuous process.

Ecuador's first attempt to export fresh flowers occurred between 1963 and 1977, but success was limited given the poor air transportation links to the U.S. market, a lack of technical know-how, and an absence of related industries.[69] The industry was revitalized in 1983, and in the two decades that followed, the area of cultivated flowers grew to approximately 5,000 hectares, 60 percent of which was occupied by roses (Expoflores).[70] Between 1997 and 2006, exports grew by 12 percent a year from $131 million to $436 million (Figure 4.1). Cut flower exports are now the country's third largest non-oil source of foreign currency, only behind bananas and shrimp.[71]

As shown in Table 4.1, the bulk of Ecuador's fresh flower exports goes to the United States, which accounts for 58 percent of total sales or 63 percent of the total volume. Russia is the second most important market, but lags well behind the United States.

---

[69] Until Ecuatoriana de Aviación, Ecuador's national carrier, scheduled a weekly flight in 1990, producers had to wait for unoccupied cargo space on passenger planes to transport their products (Arbeláez, Meléndez and León 2007).

[70] Expoflores, Ecuador's Association of Producers and Exporters of Fresh-Cut Flowers, represents about 70 percent of producers.

[71] According to Ecuador's Export and Investment Promotion Corporation statistics, non-oil exports represented $5.18 billion in 2006.

Figure 4.1. Ecuador's Exports of Fresh Flowers (1997–2006)

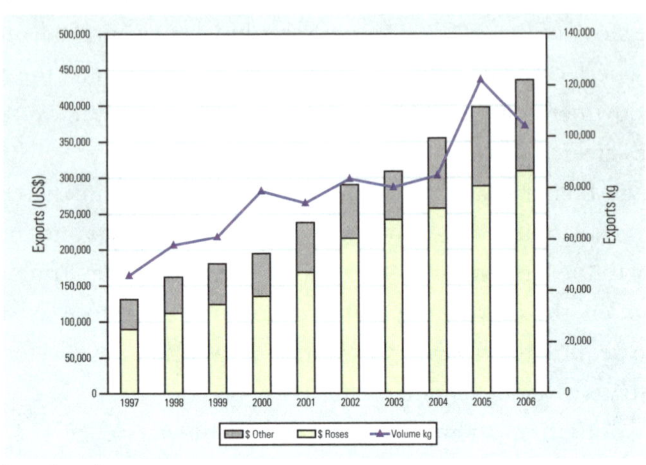

Source: Comtrade

Apart from endowments and proximity, Ecuador's cut flower exports have been benefiting from a preferential access to the U.S. market (zero tariffs), granted initially by the Andean Trade Preferences Act (ATPA) ratified in 1991 and later on extended by the Andean Trade Preferences and Drug

Table 4.1. Destination of Ecuador's Exports of Fresh Flowers (2006)

Destination	kg	$ FOB[1]	$ FOB[1] per kg	% kg	% FOB[1]
United States	65,606	254,041	3.87	63	58
Russia	12,535	59,094	4.71	12	14
Netherlands	11,014	48,115	4.37	11	11
Spain	1,863	10,940	5.87	2	3
Canada	2,483	10,803	4.35	2	2
Germany	1,752	9,021	5.15	2	2
Italy	1,537	7,960	5.18	1	2
Switzerland	1,267	6,188	4.88	1	1
Japan	517	5,283	10.23	0	1
Chile	808	3,215	3.98	1	1
Argentina	269	972	3.61	0	0
Other	4,513	20,211	4.48	4	5
Total	104,164	435,843	4.18	100	100

[1] Free on board prices.

Source: Comtrade

Eradication Act (ATPDEA) (2002). The ATPDEA was supposed to expire in June 2007, but was extended by the U.S. Congress until December 2008. Before 1991, exports of flowers were penalized with tariffs ranging from 6.4 to 6.8 percent.

Supply chain—As mentioned before, cut flowers are perishable goods; therefore, the success and the risks of the industry depend on how well integrated the different parts of the supply chain are to guarantee a delivery of a product whose quality is time sensitive. A full description of the supply chain of this industry can be found in Vega (2008). Here we simply show in Table 4.2 the length of time in different parts of the supply chain in order to provide the reader with an assessment of where the risk may be.

The table was completed using published information and complemented by a questionnaire sent to the individuals responsible for operations at major cargo agencies in Quito. As can be seen, there is a substantial variation and, therefore, uncertainty in shipping times. From the moment of harvest until the time the product arrives at the U.S. retailer, the trip can take anywhere from 44½ hours to almost 13 days.

The condition and quality of each part of the supply chain not only affect the shipping time of the product but also its transport costs. Two aspects of the supply chain that could be particularly important in this

Table 4.2. Potential to Affect Quality throughout the Supply Chain

Process	Time	Potential to Affect Quality
Post-Harvest on Farm, Ecuador	4–8 hours	Medium
Storage on Farm	12–72 hours	Low–Medium
Transportation to Cargo Agencies	1–6 hours	Medium
Storage at Cargo Agency	4 hours	Low
Palletizing, Quito	6 hours	Medium–High
Customs Clearance, Quito	0.5 hours	Low
Loading to Aircraft, Quito	1–2 hours	Medium–High
Flight UIO-MIA Nonstop	4 hours	High
Customs Clearance, Miami	4–12 hours	Low
Depalletizing, Miami	2–4 hours	High
Storage at Cargo Agency, Miami	4–72 hours	Low–Medium
Transportation to U.S. Retailer	2 hours–5 days	Medium

Source: Vega (2008).

respect are Ecuador's airport infrastructure and the degree of competition in the airline industry.

Airport Infrastructure—UIO, Quito's international airport, is located inside the city limits at about 2,814 meters above sea level and is open between 5:45 a.m. and 1:00 a.m. everyday. However, during the high season for perishables, it operates 24 hours a day. The airport has a single runway, which is 3,120 meters long. A new Quito airport is scheduled to open in 2009 and is being built in a valley 24 kilometers west of the city at 2,400 meters above sea level.

There are three major constraints affecting exports of perishables from Ecuador. First, because of the altitude, only short- to medium-range aircraft can land. For the same reasons, aircraft cannot take off fully loaded.[72] Second, there is only a limited size area for refrigerated storage, about 7,000 square meters. During high season, the area fills very rapidly, and it is not uncommon to see boxes of flowers stored on the airport's tarmac. Third, the fee structure at Ecuadorian airports has a major impact on the cost of transporting perishables. As Table 4.3 illustrates, at $2,221, UIO landing and other fees for an aircraft weighing 150 metric tons are the highest in Latin America.

Airlines—Right from the early days of the industry, guaranteeing cargo space on passenger flights has been a major problem. It was not until 1990 that the now defunct state-owned carrier *Ecuatoriana de Aviación* began to operate aircraft exclusively for cargo. Today, only a handful

Table 4.3. Estimated Landing and Other Fees at Selected Airports (March 2007)

Country	Airport Code	Landing Fees ($)	Other Fees ($)	Total ($)
Ecuador	UIO	1,661	560	2,221
Ecuador	GYE	952	305	1,257
Colombia	BOG	1,075	84	1,159
Costa Rica	SJO	60	427	487
Guatemala	GUA	40	112	152

Source: International Air Transport Association (IATA), Ecuador.

[72] A Boeing 757 jumbo jet, although suitable for operating out of UIO, is capable of transporting only up to 6,000 boxes when taking off at an altitude of 600 meters or less.

of carriers offer routes from Ecuador to the United States and Europe. In recent years integrated cargo carriers have become more important in Ecuador. An industry survey of airlines reveals that in 2005, cargo-only carriers such as Lan Cargo, Martin Air, Arrow Air, Cargolux, Tampa Cargo, and UPS together transported almost 79 percent of cargo out of Ecuador. During the peak season, firms also resort to the use of chartered cargo aircraft to overcome the transport capacity constraints.

Transport costs—A frequent claim of Ecuadorian fresh flower producers is that transportation costs are higher in Ecuador than in other countries, which significantly reduces competitiveness. The arguments supporting this contention are often anecdotal based on the "asking price" rate a freight forwarder is most likely to quote. Compared with their Colombian counterparts, producers assert that the freight rate from Ecuador is US$1.60 per kilogram, while in Colombia it is US$0.96. By contrast, IATA statistics indicate a freight rate somewhere in the middle between $1.31 and $1.38 per kilogram. Additional industry estimates suggest that transportation costs of Ecuadorian flower exports account for as much as 25 percent of the wholesale unit price of a stem in the United States and 33 percent in Europe.

To check the accuracy of these estimates, we use data from the U.S. Bureau of Census and we focus on roses, Ecuador's main flower export.[73] Table 4.4 presents the results from 2006. To control for seasonal effects, we look at freight costs in two months: February, when, due to the "Valentine day effect," demand is at its highest in the year, and August, when sales are closer to the monthly average. As can be seen, Ecuador's freight costs, measured on a per value basis, are 50 to 60 percent higher than Colombia's, a difference which cannot be explained by distance alone. The distance from Quito's to Miami's airport (1786 miles) is 17 percent higher than from Bogotá's to Miami's airport (1520 miles). Assuming an elasticity of freight to distance of approximately 0.17 (See Chapter 2, Table 2.B.4), this difference would translate into freight costs that are 2.9 percent higher,

[73] U.S. Harmonized System, 0603110060: "roses, fresh, suitable for bouquets or for ornamental purposes, not elsewhere specified or included (NESOI)."

Table 4.4. Transportation Costs of Roses from Selected Countries to the United States (2006)

Country	Distance to Main Entry U.S. Airport (Statute Miles)	February				August			
		Shipments		Freight		Shipments		Freight	
		Quantity (000 kg)	Price[1] ($/kg)	$/kg[2]	% of Price[3]	Quantity (000 kg)	Price[1] ($/kg)	$/kg[2]	% of Price[3]
Colombia	1,506	8,483	4.51	0.898	20	2,836	4.10	0.895	22
Ecuador	1,787	3,519	4.23	1.350	32	1,278	3.74	1.227	33
Guatemala	1,017	204	4.19	0.468	11	40	4.51	0.866	19
Netherlands	4,120	63	4.49	0.984	22	n/a	n/a	n/a	n/a
Kenya	7,947	33	3.46	2.746	79	3	3.53	3.030	86
Costa Rica	1,117	2	5.51	1.093	20	3	6.53	1.707	26
Israel	5,677	1	3.41	2.294	67	n/a	n/a	n/a	n/a

[1] Shipment prices equal to FOB value divided by quantity.
[2] Freight expenditures divided by the quantity shipped.
[3] Ad valorem freight expenditures.

Source: U.S. Census Bureau Foreign Trade Division Monthly Statistics.

well below the figures implied by Table 4.4. Ecuador's freight costs are also 45 percent higher than those of the Netherlands on a per value basis, even though the distance between the Amsterdam Airport and New York's JFK (the closest distribution center to the Netherlands, 3653 miles) is roughly twice that from Quito's to Miami's airport.

Ecuador's high transport cost is also suggested by the results of a regression exercise, using data for rose imports to the United States from 2000 to 2006. Controlling for differences in weight to values (or unit prices) across importers and for year and monthly effects, Ecuador's transport costs are estimated to be 15 percent higher than Colombia's and 8 percent higher than those of the Netherlands, a result that can hardly be explained on the basis of distance alone.[74]

Some of the most likely factors behind Ecuador's high transport costs were already hinted at by the previous analysis of the industry's logistic chain. That is, limited and costly airport infrastructure—including the lack of refrigeration facilities—limited competition for cargo services, and great variation and uncertainty of shipping times. Other possible sources

[74] See Vega (2008) for model specification and complete results.

of higher costs may be related to the smaller scale of Ecuador exports compared to Colombia and the Netherlands, the fee structure at Ecuadorian airports, and the substantial imbalance sustained by Ecuador in its trade with the United States, also known as the "peak load problem." When the demand for transportation services is unidirectional, freight rates are simply higher as the shipper pays for forgone capacity on either the inbound or outbound flight. When the trade imbalance is strongly positive (more exports than imports) as is the case of Ecuador, transportation costs for exports tend to be higher than for imports.

The way ahead—It seems clear from the analysis above that one can hardly overestimate the importance of transport costs for an industry such as cut flowers in Ecuador. A trade policy that focuses only on traditional, policy related trade costs would be missing the bulk of the barriers to trade and would be undercutting the country's opportunities abroad. That is particularly the case of Ecuador's exports to the United States, where a sequence of unilateral preference initiatives have eliminated tariff for Ecuador's products.

It is true that those preferences are temporary. They look particularly fragile amid the current adverse political climate to trade agreements both in the United States and in Ecuador. Yet, as important as those preferences are—particularly in the face of strong competition coming from extremely labor-intensive countries such as China—even if they were eliminated in a worst-case scenario, tariffs would remain well below freight expenditures. As mentioned earlier, tariffs before the ATPA was granted were below 7 percent, whereas our estimates in Table 4.4 put the average ad valorem freight costs at 32 to 33 percent. As we discussed in Chapter 1, if the time costs of shipping delays were included, it is more than likely that shipping costs would double, reinforcing their role as the major obstacle to Ecuador's flower exports.

Producers on the ground seem to have identified a sensible policy agenda to reduce these costs (Expoflores 2007). It speaks of more investment in airport infrastructure, and of more competition between airports and airlines, particularly through deregulation of the aviation sector. Therefore, a more balanced trade agenda that incorporates not only policy-related trade costs but also transport costs is likely to generate higher payoffs in terms of export opportunities.

Brazil: A Story of Rent Losses in Soy Exports[75]

In Chapter 1 we talked about the characteristics and requirements of LAC's comparative advantages carrying enough weight to put transport costs among the very top public policy priorities. This is arguably nowhere more evident than in the exploitation of natural resources and we can argue, in turn, that this is nowhere more evident than in soy production in Brazil.

Brazil is the world's second largest producer and exporter of soybean, after the United States. According to the United States Department of Agriculture (USDA), production in the United States reached a record 87 million tons in 2006, but the 2007 U.S. harvest is projected to be only 71 million tons.[76] Brazil's soybean output was 55 million tons in 2006 and is forecast to reach 58 million in 2007.[77] Given the potential for expanding its planted area, Brazil is expected to surpass the United States as the world's largest exporter of soybean in the future. China has been the largest importer of soybean, taking 43 percent of Brazil's export volume,[78] followed by the European Union (15 countries) with 40 percent.

Production costs—Production and land costs are much lower in the Center-West of Brazil than in the United States. Table 4.5 reveals that the farm values of one ton of soybean in this region of Brazil were indeed much lower than in the south of the country, and in the areas of Minneapolis and Davenport in the United States in the fourth quarter of 2005 and in the first quarter of 2006. On the other hand, the farm values of soybean in the south of Brazil are at about the same levels as in the United States.

The largest soybean producing and exporting area is located in the Center-West of Brazil. This area is quite a long way from the coast and comprises the states of Mato Grosso, just south of the boundaries of the Amazon rain forest, Mato Grosso do Sul, Goiás, and Distrito Federal, in the so-called Cerrado region. As has been shown, this is also the lowest-cost

[75] This section was adapted from Batista (2008), which includes not only soy, but also a case study of agricultural mechanical appliances.

[76] See Feed & Grain (2007). The primary source is USDA's World Agricultural Outlook Board (WAOB). http://www.usda.gov/oce/commodity/.

[77] Companhia Nacional de Abastecimento (2007).

[78] Exports in tons from 2004 to 2006.

Table 4.5. Farm Values of Soybean in Brazil and in the United States ($/ton)

Country	4th Qtr 2005	1st Qtr 2006
Brazil		
North Mato Grosso (Center-West)	174.28	157.86
Southeast Mato Grosso (Center-West)	174.28	157.86
South Goiás (Center-West)	184.89	180.71
North Center Paraná	214.81	206.88
Northwest Rio Grande do Sul	206.36	202.56
United States		
Minneapolis, MN	207.11	202.34
Davenport, IA	207.60	204.78

Source: USDA, *Brazil Soybean Transportation*, a quarterly publication of the transportation and marketing programs, Transportation Services Branch, August 10, 2006, www.ams.usda.gov/tmdtsb/grain.

soybean producing area in Brazil. In 2006, 14 million tons of soybean were moved from these states to Brazilian ports for export. This was almost 60 percent of that region's output. The soybean transported to the ports from Mato Grosso only totaled approximately 10 million tons in the same year.

The ports of Santos and Paranaguá accounted for 28 and 16 percent, respectively, of the soybean exported from Brazil in 2006. The ports of Rio Grande (RS) and São Francisco do Sul (SC) accounted for 14 and 12 percent, respectively. Considering that trucks account for about 60 percent of general cargo transport in Brazil, and bearing in mind that 75 percent of exports of soybean take place in the months from April to September and 40 percent in the three months from May to July, it is possible to have an idea of the traffic flow generated by exports of this crop on already very busy roads crossing the states of São Paulo and Paraná. Assuming that exports of soybean departing from the ports of Manaus (1584 tons) and Santarém (954 tons) are originally from the state of Mato Grosso, it is possible to estimate that about 7.3 million tons of soybean had to be transported along approximately 2200 km from this state only to the ports of Santos and Paranaguá in 2006.[79]

[79] It is possible to estimate roughly the number of truck journeys used to transport soybean from Mato Grosso to the ports of Santos and Paranaguá in 2006. Given that a truck carries on average 35 tons of soybean, 927 truck journeys per day were necessary in the months from May to July, and 811 trucks per day in April, August and September.

Table 4.6. Transportation Costs from Farms to Ports ($/ton)

	North of Mato Grosso to Paranaguá	Minneapolis to the Gulf	Davenport to the Gulf
	by truck	by truck and barge	by truck and barge
1st Qtr 2005	69.96	7.58 + 8.42 = 26.00	7.58 + 18.16 = 25.74
2nd Qtr 2005	79.07	7.82 + 8.93 = 26.75	7.82 + 14.67 = 22.49
3rd Qtr 2005	80.67	8.90 + 28.88 = 37.78	8.90 + 23.63 = 32.53
4th Qtr 2005	80.86	10.06 + 36.71 = 46.77	10.06 + 30.91 = 40.97
1st Qtr 2006	84.65	9.42 + 25.38 = 34.80	9.42 + 21.42 = 30.84

Source: USDA, *Brazil Soybean Transportation,* a quarterly publication of the transportation and marketing programs, Transportation Services Branch, August 10, 2006, www.ams.usda.gov/tmdtsb/grain.

Domestic freight costs—Table 4.6 clearly reveals that the transportation costs from the cheapest producing area in Brazil to the main port in Paraná by truck are much higher than the cost of bringing down the soybean produced around Minneapolis and Davenport by truck and barge, along the Mississippi River, to the Gulf ports in the United States.

The high cost of transportation from farms in Mato Grosso to the port of Paranaguá is partly because of the long distance, but also due to the lack of intermodal competition. In Mato Grosso, the rail system is almost nonexistent. As a result, grains have to be moved by trucks either directly to ports or to railway or waterway transfer terminals far away from the farms in the north of the state. The high cost of transporting soybean by trucks is exacerbated by the poor condition of the roads. In point of fact, both the highways from the north of the state to the transfer terminal of the Madeira River in Porto Velho (RO) (BR-364) and to the Amazon River Port of Santarém-Para (BR-163) are still unpaved.[80] Although paving these roads is said to be a major federal government priority, environmental restrictions and lack of funds have been inhibiting this project.

On the other hand, more than half of the U.S. soybean exports traverse some portion of the Mississippi River System. Bulk transportation costs for barges do not increase the farm price that much of American

---

[80] ". . . only 12% of the 999,857 miles of Brazilian roads are paved. The condition of the paved roads varies across the country, with half the paved roads ranging from passable to very bad," Boletim Estatístico, Confederação Nacional do Transporte, December 2005.

Table 4.7. Soybean Costs at Ports in Brazil and in the United States ($/ton)

Country	4th Qtr 2005	1st Qtr 2006
Brazil		
Rio Grande from Northwest RS	219.56 (6%)	216.10 (6%)
Santos from South Goiás	227.45 (19%)	223.20 (19%)
Paranaguá from North Center Paraná	236.06 (9%)	226.29 (9%)
Paranaguá from North Mato Grosso	255.14 (32%)	242.51 (35%)
United States		
Gulf of Mexico from Davenport, IA	248.57 (16.5%)	235.62 (13%)
Gulf of Mexico from Minneapolis, MN	253.88 (18%)	237.14(15%)

Note: The share of domestic transportation in soybean costs at the port is shown in parentheses.

Source: USDA, *Brazil Soybean Transportation*, a quarterly publication of the transportation and marketing programs, Transportation Services Branch, August 10, 2006, www.ams.usda.gov/tmdtsb/grain.

soybean.[81] Indeed, transportation costs, including trucks and barges, from Minneapolis and Davenport were between 13 and 18 percent of the Gulf price, whereas the truck costs from north of Mato Grosso were between 32 and 35 percent of the price at Paranaguá.[82]

Table 4.7 adds the farm values, shown in Table 4.5, to the domestic transportation costs from the main areas of production to the main ports of soybean export, shown in Table 4.6. It is clear that the cost of transporting soybean to the port of Paranaguá more than erodes the farm cost advantage of the cheapest producing area of Brazil. Minneapolis and Davenport soybean at the Gulf ports was cheaper than the soybean from the north of Mato Grosso at the Paranaguá port in 2005/2006.

However, the costs of soybean at the ports of Rio Grande, Paranaguá, and Santos from the northwest of Rio Grande do Sul, north center of Paraná, and south of Goiás, respectively, were lower than at the Gulf ports of the United States. Transportation costs were decisive for this price

[81] According to the USDA, the Mississippi barge transportation rates can be further reduced through a modernization of the locks on the river system, avoiding splitting of tows, and thus allowing cuts in transit times (Mark Ash, Janet Livezey, and Erik Dohlman, *Soybean Backgrounder*, Electronic Outlook Report from the Economic Research Service, USDA, OCS-2006-01, April 2006).

[82] The soybean price at Paranaguá is used by traders as the general reference price for the Brazilian soybean premium compared to Chicago stock exchange prices.

Table 4.8. Ocean Freight Rates for Shipping Soybean ($/Metric Ton)

	To Shanghai	To Hamburg	
From	2006	2005	2006
	1st Qtr	4th Qtr	1st Qtr
Santos	50.13	56.73	39.51
Paranaguá	49.13	55.73	38.51
Rio Grande	48.63	55.23	37.06
Gulf of Mexico	35.71	22.81	19.53

Source: USDA, *Brazil Soybean Transportation,* a quarterly publication of the transportation and marketing programs, Transportation Services Branch, August 10, 2006, www.ams.usda.gov/tmdtsb/grain.

advantage, as they accounted for only 6 percent, 9 percent, and 19 percent of soybean costs at the ports of Rio Grande, Paranaguá, and Santos, respectively, in 2005–2006.

International freight costs—Brazil's competitive position in soybean exports is further deteriorated once ocean freight rates are taken into account, as the examples of freight rates from Brazil and from the United States to Shanghai (China) and Hamburg (Germany) in Table 4.8 clearly illustrate.

Ocean freight rates for transporting soybean from Brazil depend, among other things, on the export volumes of soybean and iron ore. The availability of vessels tends to increase, relative to the volume of soybean exports, as exports of iron ore decline, reducing the freight rates.

Table 4.9 shows soybean costs from Brazil and from the United States in Shanghai and in Hamburg. Note that the shares of transportation costs in landed costs both in Shanghai and in Hamburg tend to be higher for soybean from Brazil than from the United States, especially for soybean produced in the Center-West region of Brazil.

Examining the market shares of Brazil and the United States in imports of soybean in different countries, it seems that Brazil is more competitive than the United States in European countries and became more competitive in China in 2006 (Table 4.10). On the other hand, the United States is still more competitive in Japan and totally dominates the import markets of Canada and Mexico. Ocean freight costs still maintain

Table 4.9. Landed Costs and Shares of Transportation Costs ($/Ton in the 1st Qtr 2006)

To	Shanghai	Share	Hamburg	Share
From Brazil				
Northwest Rio Grande do Sul-Rio Grande	264.73	(23%)	253.16	(20%)
South Goiás-Santos	273.33	(34%)	262.71	(31%)
North Center Paraná-Paranaguá	275.42	(25%)	264.79	(22%)
North Mato Grosso-Paranaguá	291.64	(46%)	281.02	(44%)
From the United States				
Davenport-Gulf	271.33	(25%)	255.15	(20%)
Minneapolis-Gulf	272.85	(26%)	256.67	(21%)

Note: The share of transportation costs in landed costs is shown in parentheses.

Source: Brazil Soybean Transportation, USDA August 10, 2006.

Table 4.10. Market Shares of Brazil and the U.S. in Selected Importing Countries

	Importers						
Exporters	China		Japan		Germany		Netherlands
	2005	2006	2005	2006	2005	2006	2005
Brazil	30%	41%	13%	9%	59%	51%	71%
United States	42%	35%	75%	80%	28%	36%	18%

Based on imports by countries of HS 120100.
Source: Comtrade, United Nations.

U.S. soybeans' competitive standing in neighboring countries, Mexico and Canada, where the United States supplies between 98 and 100 percent of these countries' soybean imports.

Tariffs—Soybean imports enter countries of the European Union, Japan, and Taiwan free of import tariffs. China charges an MFN tariff between 0 and 3 percent[83] (average 2.4 percent according to UNCTAD), but Brazilian soybean pays no import tariff. Mexico imports free of import tax from February 1 to July 31, but charges 15 percent MFN tariff from August 1 to January 31. Brazil and Mexico's trade agreement (ACE 53) gives

[83] These tariffs refer to the group of products classified at the 6-digit level of the Harmonized System (HS 120100).

a preference of 80 percent of the Mexican tariff to Brazil. Chile and Peru have an ad valorem MFN tariff of 8 percent and 4 percent, respectively.

The case of the Caramuru Group—The Caramuru Group is a large exporter and manufacturer of soybean in Brazil, processing 3500 tons of this grain per day, producing lethicin (900 tons/month), soy oil (600 tons/day) and biodiesel (300 tons/day). It is also a corn manufacturer, processing 2054 tons of this grain per day, and operates grain-handling facilities such as storage facilities for 1.6 million tons, facilities for load transfer at an intermodal railway-waterway terminal in Pederneiras (SP), on the banks of the Tietê and Paraná Rivers, a waterway terminal in Anhembi (SP), and port terminals in Tubarão (ES) and Santos (SP). It employs 2150 workers.

Because trade costs vary enormously according to the area of production, we focus here on trade costs associated with production in the north of the state of Mato Grosso, which is the greatest and lowest-cost producing area. In the state of Mato Grosso, production is concentrated in the area around the city of Sorriso. From this area, there are alternative routes to transport this crop to a port for export. For example, grains are carried by trucks (as the rail system is almost nonexistent in Mato Grosso): (i) directly to the ports of Santos (SP), Paranaguá (PR), or Santarém (PA); (ii) to Porto Velho (RO), then on barges to the port of Itacoatiara (AM); (iii) to the railway terminal in Alto Araguaia in the south of the state of Mato Grosso, near the border with the states of Goiás and Mato Grosso do Sul, and from there to the port of Santos on railway; or (iv) to the railway terminal in Maringa, in the state of Paraná, and from there to the port of Paranaguá on railway. All these routes are quite expensive, as transport costs account for about one-third of the FOB price of the product, whatever the selected route.

Once the soybean reaches a port in Brazil, it is necessary to add the costs of stocking, loading and unloading, and all the legal rates at the port of embarkation. The port of Santos was selected, since it is the largest exporter of Brazilian soybean.[84] At the port of Santos the product stays on

---

[84] Paranaguá used to be the top Brazil soybean export port, but lost its leadership to Santos when it banned genetically modified soy passing through the port from October 2003 to April 2006.

Table 4.11. Trade Costs from Brazil to China: Sorriso-Shanghai, 2007

	US$/Ton	% of Farm Price
Farm Price	206.00	100.0
Transport to Santos	101.59	49.3
Port Costs	7.00	3.4
Transport to China	50.00	24.3
Other Costs*	3.10	1.5
TOTAL	367.69	178.5

* Legal, contracts, and information costs.

average seven days. The Caramuru Group estimates that these port costs total US$7.00/ton in Santos.

The cost from Santos to China is US$50 per ton (of which 90 percent is for the freight and 10 percent for insurance) and sixty tons of soybeans are embarked per vessel. The distance is 18,734 km and the average time is 37 days. There are no regular lines, so transportation is taken by tramp ships. Among other things, freight costs depend on the export volume of other commodities, especially iron ore in this case. But the main structural problem appears to be the low levels of dry cargo imports to fill bulk carriers on the way to Brazil. This seems to raise significantly Brazil's ocean freight rates for grains. Table 4.11 sums up all these costs. It should be noted that trade costs are equivalent to 178.5 percent of the farm price.

According to Caramuru, trade costs could be reduced through investments in the transportation infrastructure. The supply of railway services is low in the existing lines. Much has to be done to improve the efficiency of the railways. The Brazilian railway system carries 21 billion tons per kilometer-year, compared to 2700 billion tons in the United States, and the average speed of trains for load transportation in Brazil is still 25 km per hour, compared to 64 km per hour in the United States.[85] Extending the railway lines into Mato Grosso would help to reduce transportation costs,

[85] Associação Nacional de Transportes Ferroviários and CIA *World Factbook*; both were primary sources quoted in Veja, Veja.com., Edicão 2020, August 8, 2007: http://veja.abril.com.br/080807/p_084.shtm.

but not the efficiency of the system. The Paranaíba-Tietê-Paraná waterways could also be improved through investments in protecting bridge pillars and in dredging the rivers to allow larger vessels. Unpaved highways ought to be paved, paved highways ought to be kept in good condition, but toll roads are expensive for transporting grains. Ocean freight rates could be reduced through investments in harbor dredging that could allow larger ships into the ports.

Beyond traditional trade policy—All in all, when transporting goods to ports eats away as much as 49 percent of the producers' revenue and when overall costs (internal and external) of delivering goods to one of the producers' major clients is as high as 79 percent of the producers' price, one can be sure that there is something wrong about a trade policy that focuses only on traditional market access, the more so when tariffs are well below the ad valorem transport costs of even the most efficient routes. As argued in Chapter 1, natural resource goods are intrinsically transport intensive because they are "heavy goods." In this context, an inefficient and dysfunctional logistic chain can cause as much havoc to the opportunities to trade and their related gains as the type of protectionist regimes that were common in LAC until the late 1980s.

Argentina: A Story of New Opportunities in Farm Equipment Facing Transport Constraints[86]

Argentina's farm equipment industry has been experiencing a revival in the last four years, driven by the commodity boom, the currency devaluation and the economy's fast recovery. Sales of tractors, seeders, combine harvesters and miscellaneous agricultural appliances grew at an annual average rate of 19 percent in 2002–2006, reaching US$346 million in 2006. Exports have also been brisk, growing by 19 percent annually in the same period. As can be seen in Figure 4.2, Venezuela accounts for the bulk of Argentina's farm equipment exports, followed well behind by Brazil, Chile and Uruguay.

---

[86] This section was adapted from Sicra (2008), which includes not only farm equipment, but also a case study of powdered milk.

Figure 4.2. Direction of Argentinean Exports of Farm Equipment, US$ (2007)*

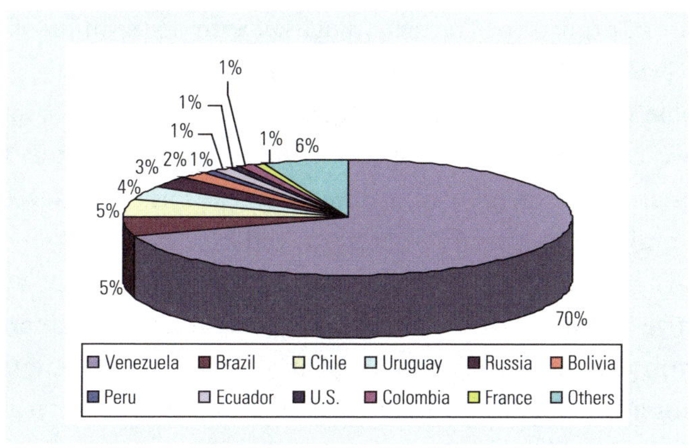

* January to July.
Source: Sistema Informático María (SIM) on line de la Aduana Argentina. http://www.afip.gov.ar/aduana/sim/.

Venezuela's preeminence as a market is explained to a great extent by the signing of a number of bilateral agreements between the Venezuelan and Argentinean governments, whereby the former sells oil in exchange for a number of previously agreed Argentinean products, which range from agricultural to capital goods, including farm equipment. The first agreement was signed in 2004, but it was only in 2005 that farm equipment was included in the exchange list.[87] In the latest version of the agreement, signed in 2007, Venezuela committed to buy US$155 million worth of equipment, approximately 30 percent of the industry's sales.

It didn't take long, though, for this fast growth of exports to test the limits of Argentina's transport infrastructure. The logistic difficulties of the farm equipment firms became clear in a series of interviews with exporters, business associations, freight forwarders and civil servants.

[87] Convenio Integral de Cooperación entre la República Argentina y la República Bolivariana de Venezuela, April 6, 2004. Farm equipment was included by the Acuerdo Complementario al Convenio Básico sobre Cooperación Económica, Industrial, Tecnológica y Comercial en el Área de Provisión de Implementos y Maquinaria Agrícola entre la República Argentina y la República Bolivariana de Venezuela; Brasilia, September 29, 2005. See Sicra (2008) for more details.

Shipping capacity—According to the interviews, farm equipment exporters face a shortage of cargo capacity, which is particularly acute in the case of exports to Venezuela, a market with no tradition of farm equipment exports. Exporters to this Andean country struggle to find space available in commercial lines, which do not offer a direct route between the two countries. Large, self-propelled equipment such as tractors and harvesters face even more difficulties since car companies take all the cargo space available in specialized, "roll-on/roll-off" ships.

These problems were ameliorated to a large extent by an opportune initiative led by CFMA (Cámara de Fabricantes de Maquinaria Agrícola), the farm equipment business association, which has prompted exporters to consolidate their cargo and to negotiate jointly the chartering of a number of ships, which has not only alleviated the cargo restrictions, but also contributed to lowering freight costs to an average of 8 percent of the CIF value of exports.

Another hurdle that exporters have to face is the availability and costs of containers. Shipping companies usually rent containers, but the substantial growth of Argentina's exports has led to a shortage in certain periods of the year, with exporters scrambling to find an alternative supply. This affects not only exports to Venezuela, but also to other destinations such as Colombia and Europe. In the case of Venezuela, though, exporters face extra costs since the companies that rent containers are reluctant to leave them in this country, an exporter of bulk products. Exporters are consequently forced to pay the extra cost of shipping containers to ports with greater traffic such as Houston.

Port capacity—Buenos Aires, for reasons related to its location, the depth of its cargo berths and available infrastructure, is the busiest port in Argentina, a characteristic that has been accentuated by the recent export boom. Exporters complain about issues that are typical of port congestion such as an increase in loading times, difficulties in road access to the port, the high tariffs of its services and the lack of available facilities to store and consolidate the cargo. In the specific case of Venezuela, CFMA has also found a way to alleviate these constraints by moving shipping operations to Puerto de Zárate, located in the north of Buenos Aires province. This port is smaller than Buenos Aires, but is closer to the factories and CFMA was able to negotiate the services at a lower rate.

Customs delays—Overland shipping to neighboring countries such as Bolivia, Uruguay and Chile faces some difficulties in terms of the availability of container trucks, but the more pressing problem is the delays at the border crossings, which are seen as particularly acute in the case of Chile (weather-related closings) and Uruguay (blockades imposed by what has become known as the "*papelera* conflict").[88] A common problem that is viewed as affecting shipping to all countries is the delays caused, on the one hand, by the usual lack of documentation of shippers that want to cross the border, and, on the other, by the perceived inefficiencies of the customs work, including the duplicity of controls on both sides of the border.

The costs to export—To have a more precise estimate of the trade costs that affect producers of farm equipment in Argentina, we look at a sample of ocean shipments of four types of equipment to Mexico and Venezuela. Two of them (disc harrows and seeders for direct seeding) are shipped in containers and the other two (tractors and harvesters) are shipped in the ship's cargo area. We also look at the shipment of tractors overland to Chile.

Table 4.12 presents the trade cost estimates for the joint shipment of the four products to Mexico and Venezuela, totaling US$219,000 (FOB). The methodology and the disaggregated data are available in Sicra (2008). As can be seen, transport costs, including domestic and international freight, amount to 10.6 percent of the CIF value, the bulk of it explained by the ocean freight. Other trade costs related to ports, documents and customs amount to 3.8 percent. Overall, the costs to export reach 14.4 percent of the CIF value in a context where traditional policy-related trade costs

---

[88] Since December 2004, Argentinean activists opposed to the construction of paper mills across the border in Uruguay have intermittently blocked the bridge that joins the two countries.

Table 4.12. Average Trade Costs of Exporting Farm Equipment to Venezuela and Mexico, Ocean Shipping (2007)

Costs	US$	% FOB Price	% CIF Price
Factory Price	219,000	95.3	85.6
Inland Freight	2,200	1.0	0.9
Cargo Consolidation at Port	2,180	0.9	0.8
Customs	400	0.2	0.2
Documents Required by Importer	800	0.3	0.3
Importer's Inspection	640	0.3	0.2
Port Expenses	753	0.3	0.3
Maritime Agency	1,488	0.6	0.6
Letter of Credit	561	0.2	0.2
Other Expenses	1,870	0.8	0.7
Subtotal FOB	229,892	100.0	89.8
Insurance	1,122	0	0.4
Freight	24,950	0	9.7
Total CIF	255,964	0	100.0

Source: Sicra (2008).

are zero or very close to zero. In the case of land freight (Table 4.13), transport costs, as expected, are considerably lower (5 percent of the CIF value) reflecting, inter alia, the shorter distance to Chile. When added to the other export expenses, trade costs amount to 8.6 percent of the CIF value, not as high as in ocean shipping to Mexico and Venezuela, but, again, a magnitude that dwarfs tariffs and non-tariff barriers.[89]

Overall, Argentina's case study draws attention to at least three often forgotten and important issues. First, the export of new products to new markets often involve logistic requirements that can play a key role in consolidating and expanding the initial gains. Second, private sector associations, as was the case of CAFMA, can play a key role in overcoming logistic constraints, with response times that can be far superior to that of governments. Finally, as shown in the other cases and throughout the chapters of this report, non-policy trade costs, particularly transport costs, tend to be a much more important obstacle to trade than tariffs and non-tariff barriers, the more so when it comes to trade within the region.

[89] ALADI data for 2005 puts the weighted ad valorem tariffs (HS 87012020) at 0.04 percent.

Table 4.13. Trade Costs of Exporting Farm Equipment to Chile, Overland Shipping (2007)

Costs	US$	% FOB Price	% CIF Price
Factory Price	45,000	95.88	91.3
Inland Freight	450	0.96	0.9
Cargo Consolidation at Port	500	1.07	1.0
Customs	100	0.21	0.2
Documents Required by Importer	200	0.43	0.4
Importer's Inspection	160	0.34	0.3
Letter of Credit	115	0.25	0.2
Other Expenses	410	0.87	0.8
Subtotal FOB	46,935	100.00	95.3
Insurance	230	0	0.5
Cost of Customs Delays	150	0.3	0.3
International Freight	1,950	0	4.0
Total CIF	**49,265**	0	100.0

Source: Sicra (2008).

Mexico: A Story about Textiles, Competition, Proximity and Delays at the Border[90]

This case study focuses on one of the leading Mexican textile firms, which has its plants in the central area of the country. Firm Y, whose real name is omitted here because of a confidentiality agreement, is vertically integrated, producing linen, other fabrics and apparel. It employs approximately 10,000 workers and began to export in 1986. Currently, it exports 50 percent of its output, half indirectly through *maquiladoras,* to the United States. The other half is exported directly to South America (40 percent, mainly to Colombia), to the United States (40 percent) and Europe (20 percent, mainly to France and Spain). The firm has plans to expand its exports to Central America, by becoming a regional supplier of textiles to *maquiladoras* throughout the region.[91]

With this profile, firm Y has long, first-hand experience with both importing and shipping goods abroad, from and to different markets, and

[90] This section is an edited and shortened version of Dussel Peters (2008), which includes not only textiles (denim), but also case studies of cotton and two pharmaceutical products.

[91] See Cárdenas Castro and Dussel Peters (2007).

a clear view of the costs and times involved. We focus on the firm's logistic chain when importing its main input—cotton—and exporting one of its main products—denim.

Importing cotton—Mexico is a major importer of cotton, most of it from the United States. In 2006, the country imported US$490 million, 99 percent of which came from the United States. Firm Y is one of the main direct importers of the product and, after assessing a number of options, has decided to take responsibility for its transportation from Nuevo Laredo, Texas, to its plants in central Mexico.[92]

The firm has an annual purchasing program, updated every month, for the types of cotton it needs and, one week before receiving the product, it starts the procedures to clear customs and for having the right type of transportation available (tractor trailers). From the moment the cotton arrives in Nuevo Laredo to its delivery in Central Mexico, it takes, on average, 2 to 6 days. Up to 84 percent of the time is spent on customs procedures, including phytosanitary inspections in the United States and Mexico and fumigation in Mexico. Actual transportation takes only one day. Leaving time costs aside, the whole process increases the price of the product by approximately 6 percent, 77 percent of which is explained by freight expenditures and the rest by the customs requirements.

Firm Y has also explored alternatives such as rail freight, which, given the relatively high weight and volume of the product, could mean lower costs. In practice, though, rail transportation turns out to be more expensive and more time consuming due to the limitations of Mexico's rail infrastructure. The closest cargo transfer station to Y's factories is 80 km away, requiring further additional land transportation that would increase transport time to five days. The company has also explored different scenarios to reduce non-transport trade costs, looking particularly at the duplication of phytosanitary controls at the border. The most favorable scenario would be to eliminate all Mexico's phytosanitary controls, leaving only the U.S. inspection in place. This would reduce overall trade costs by 16 percent and would reduce the time spent at the border to just one day.

---

[92] More specifically, the imported cotton is defined as cotton without nuggets, HS 520100.

Figure 4.3. Market Share of the U.S. Imports of Denim, Mexico and Selected Countries

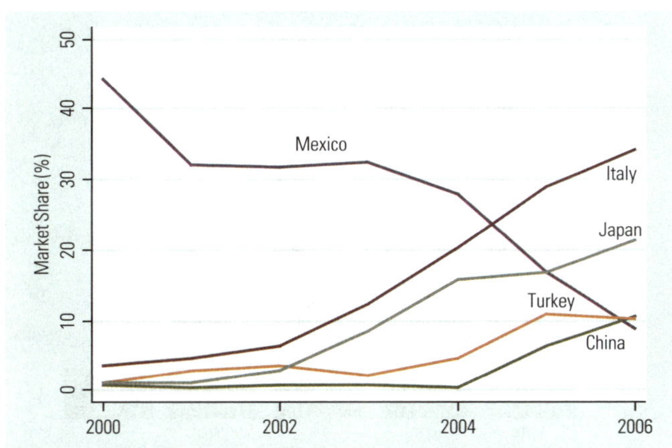

Note: Denim is defined as HS 520942.
Source: U.S. Census Bureau.

Exporting denim—Since the implementation of NAFTA, Mexico has become a major supplier to the United States of denim, a type of cotton textile known for its use in blue jeans and other clothing. Taking advantage of the combination of proximity, low labor costs and low tariffs, Mexico's share of the U.S. market jumped from negligible to a peak of 50 percent in 1999. Since then, however, it has been declining steadily, losing ground, on the one hand, to high-quality (high unit price) producers such as Italy and Japan, and, on the other, to low-cost producers such as China and Turkey (see Figure 4.3).

Mexico's loss of market share is taking place despite the relatively low trade costs of its exports to the United States. As shown in Figure 4.4, Mexico faces tariffs that are close to 7 percentage points lower than Turkey's and China's and has also substantially lower freight costs than all other competitors, except for China, whose transport costs, despite the difference in proximity and similarity of unit prices, are not that much higher than Mexico's. Overall, though, China's trade costs are four times that of Mexico.

Notwithstanding this inhospitable competitive environment, firm Y's performance in this product does not appear to have been affected.

Figure 4.4. Trade Costs of Denim Exports to the U.S., Mexico and Selected Countries (2006)

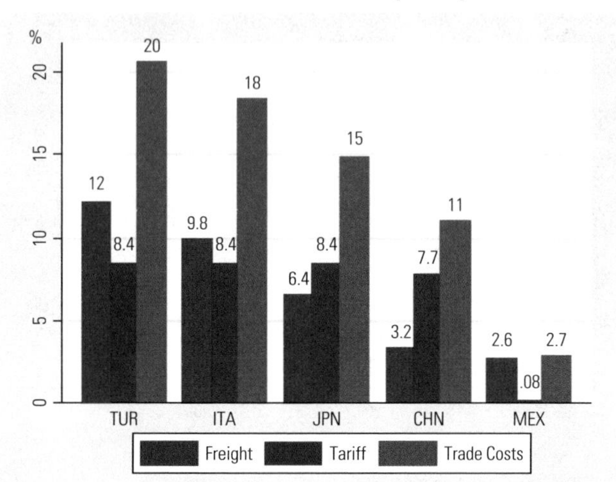

Note: Trade costs are tariff plus freight. Denim is defined as HS 520942.
Source: U.S. Census Bureau.

With decades of export experience to the United States, Europe and Latin America, denim exports of firm Y have shown healthy growth and its output grew by approximately 40 percent in 2007.

Table 4.14 shows the cost and time involved in exporting firm Y's denim to the United States (Uvalde, Texas). As with importing cotton,

Table 4.14. Trade Costs of Exporting Denim to the U.S., Road Transportation

Costs	% of Total Costs	Costs per Truck (US$)	Time
Transport Costs to the Border	34.2	632.74	
Customs Fees and Paperwork	11.3	209.74	18 Hours
Total Costs on Mexico's Side	45.6	842.48	
Customs Fees and Paperwork	13.0	240.00	1 to 3 Days
Transport Costs (Laredo-Uvalde, TX)	41.4	766.00	7 Hours
Total Costs on the U.S. Side	54.4	1,006.00	
Total Costs "Door to Door"	100.0	1,848.48	3 to 4 Days
Total Costs per Yard		0.08	
Door-to-Door Price per Yard		2.14	

Source: Interview with firm Y in 2007.

most of the time involved in the operation is spent on customs procedures. Freight accounts, on average, for 25 percent of the time, but for 75 percent of the costs. Overall, trade costs account for 3.7 percent of the delivery price; an estimate that looks modest, but that does not include the time costs arising, for instance, from delays at the border.

Using Hummels and Schaur's time cost estimates discussed in Chapter 1, each day spent at the border imposes a cost to denim exports that is equivalent to an ad valorem tariff of 0.8 percent. A three-day delay at the border—a figure that according to firm Y is not uncommon—increases ad valorem trade costs by 2.4 percentage points. If we add the time spent in transportation, the total time cost would amount to 3.2 percent, taking overall trade costs to 6.9 percent of the delivery price. In an industry where, as shown, competitive pressures are hard to underestimate and whose profit margins, according to firm Y, are between 6 to 8 percent, non-policy trade costs look far from negligible, particularly in a scenario where tariffs are already zero or close to zero.

Taken as a whole, this case study tells a cautionary tale about the importance of non-policy trade costs for countries where proximity, interacting with local endowments, plays a key role in their comparative and competitive advantages. The signing of NAFTA brought a sharp reduction in the policy trade costs of Mexico's exports to the U.S. market, which combined with proximity and low labor costs, opened vast export opportunities in labor-intensive, time-sensitive goods such as denim. After an initial export boom, though, the new realities of the world market were quickly brought into play. Faced with strong competition from extremely labor-abundant, low-transport-cost countries such as China and by technologically sophisticated countries such as Japan, Mexico's share of denim imports to the United States began to decline rapidly.

In such a scenario, where every advantage counts, proximity plays a vital, strategic role. As discussed earlier, this is not only about the geographical distance between countries, but also about the time taken to cover this distance. The story of firm Y shows that there are important actions that Mexico can take to maximize this advantage, particularly with regard to border delays. It also draws attention to the fact that in a world where production is increasingly fragmented, governments should pay attention to the trade costs of both exporting and importing goods. Firm Y's costs to import cotton are as high as 19 percent, even though the product is coming from the neighboring United States. These high costs end up compromising the competitiveness of downstream products such as denim and here the story is not only about border delays, but also about the limitation of Mexico's rail infrastructure. Gone are the days when promoting exports was only about market access.

References

Arbeláez, M., M. Meléndez and N. León. 2007. *The Emergence of New Successful Export Activities in Colombia.* Bogota: Fedesarrollo.

Ash, Mark, Janet Livezey and Erik Dohlman. 2006 (April). *Soybean Backgrounder.* Washington, D.C.: United States Department of Agriculture, Electronic Outlook Report from the Economic Research Service.

Batista, Chami Jorge. 2008. *Trade Costs for Brazilian Exporting Goods: Two Case Studies.* Washington, D.C.: Inter-American Development Bank.

Cárdenas Castro, Lorena, and Enrique Dussel Peters. 2007. México y China en la cadena hilo-textil-confección en el mercado de Estados Unidos. *Comercio Exterior* 57.

Companhia Nacional de Abastecimento. 2007. Acompanhamento da Safra Brasileira, Grãos, Décimo Levantamento. www.conab.gov.br, accessed August 2007.

Dussel Peters, Enrique. 2008. Los costos de transporte de en las exportaciones Mexicanas. Background Paper for the IDB Report, Unclogging the Veins of Latin America and the Caribbean. Washington, D.C.: Inter-American Development Bank.

Expoflores. 2007. Electronic Communication, Fairfax, September 21.

Feed & Grain. 2007. Reduction in U.S. Soybean Crop Creates Price Spike. University of Illinois at Urbana-Champaign, http://www.feedandgrain.com/web/online/NEWS/Reduction-in-US-Soybean-Crop-Creates-Price-Spike/1$676, accessed August 24, 2007.

Sicra, Ricardo. 2008. *Costos de Exportación en Argentina Dos casos de Estudio.* Washington, D.C.: Inter-American Development Bank.

USDA (U.S. Department of Agriculture). 2006 (August). *Brazil Soybean Transportation.* A quarterly publication of the transportation and marketing programs, Transportation Services Branch. Washington, D.C.: USDA.

Vega, Henry. 2008. Transportation Costs of Fresh Flowers: A Comparison across Major Exporting Countries. Washington, D.C.: Inter-American Development Bank.

Veja.com, Edicao 2020. 2007 (August).

Chapter 5

Conclusions: Expanding the Integration Agenda beyond Tariffs

This report is about refocusing LAC's trade agenda. It is about bringing the long neglected non-policy trade costs to the center stage of the policy debate. Trade policy in the region has been traditionally focused on removing tariffs and non-tariff barriers. There is little doubt that these barriers were "the elephant in LAC's living room" in the late 1980s and the emphasis on their removal was not only warranted but also inexorable, given the prevailing political incentives and the constraints in terms of administrative resources.

However, one troubling legacy of this liberalization *juggernaut* was the neglect of other, less visible, and therefore politically unattractive, costs that matter a great deal for trade. All the issues that are generally known as "trade facilitation" were squeezed out of the region's trade agenda, particularly those related to transportation costs.

We argue in this report that if this neglect was not too costly in the late 1980s, because of the sheer magnitude of the policy barriers, it has rapidly become so in the last two decades. A combination of factors has given transportation costs an unprecedented strategic importance to the region: the very success of the trade reforms—which has drastically altered the relative importance of policy versus non-policy barriers—and the rapid transformations of the world economy, above all the growing fragmentation of production and time sensitiveness of trade and the emergence of vastly labor-intensive and resource-scarce economies.

The strength of this argument is evident when we explore a large dataset on freight and tariffs in LAC and in the United States. In Chapter 1, we show, first, that for most LAC countries transport costs are significantly higher than tariffs, for both import and exports and especially for intraregional trade, a dominance that is even more overwhelming when the time costs of shipping are included. Second, the region spends more on transport costs than the United States, Europe or Asia. Third, trends in LAC's transport costs bring mixed news in terms of convergence to the developed world's levels. We see convergence in ocean freight, but a growing gap when it comes to the increasingly important airfreight. Finally, we show that the region's exports to key markets such as the United States are on average more "transport intensive" than those of its competitors, a fact that reflects the region's increasing reliance on two key drivers of its comparative advantages: natural resources and proximity to the world's largest markets.

In Chapter 2, we take a careful look at the level and determinants of LAC's transport costs and the first thing we see is that the region's shipping costs are considerably higher than those observed in developed economies and that composition plays a key role in explaining these differences. The goods that the region imports or exports, particularly the latter, are considerably "heavier" than those of the United States or Europe. This means that LAC, because of the goods it trades, is destined to pay more for transportation (on an ad valorem basis), whatever the quality of its infrastructure. Rather than viewing this fact as inevitable and moving on to discuss infrastructure, we view it as reinforcing the point made earlier about transport intensity: composition alone attaches a strategic importance to LAC's transport costs.

Composition, however, does not tell the whole story. Once we net out its influence, we see that factors that are related to the efficiency of the infrastructure explain the bulk of the difference between LAC and its developed partners. Distance generally plays only a minor role and this only adds to the urgency and importance of improving the region's logistic chains. If distance does not matter that much, advantages such as proximity to large markets can be easily overcome if the region's transport infrastructure does not keep up with that of its competitors.

But what exactly should be the government priorities in tackling this infrastructure gap? As far as we can see—and we do not have the whole picture because we didn't look at transport costs behind the borders, except for the case studies in Chapter 4—improving the efficiency of ports and airports, which generally explains about 40 percent of the differences in shipping costs between LAC and the United States and Europe, appears to offer the highest returns. For instance, our estimations suggest that improving port efficiency to the level of the United States could reduce ad valorem freight rates of LAC's imports by an average of 20 percent.

Increasing competition among shipping companies also appears to be a promising route. Our estimates suggest that the potential for gains in this area are considerably more modest than those that relate to infrastructure efficiency. Yet, given the difficulties in measuring competition in the shipping industry, particularly in airfreight, those results should not be read as an endorsement of the status quo; certainly not of the current state of government regulations in the region.

Clearly, there are costly distortions being perpetrated against competition in the airline industry, the result of an anachronistic web of bilateral air service agreements. Analysts often use the expression "spaghetti bowl" to describe the myriad of trade agreements governing trade in goods in the region. Yet, when compared to the airline industry regulations, particularly in terms of the costs of distortions, the spaghetti bowl of trade agreements appears to be just a side dish. Brazil's recent initiative of proposing an "open air agreement" for South America certainly points in the right direction.[93]

A less intuitive government priority that also comes out of Chapter 2 concerns the role of import tariffs in raising transport costs. Higher tariff means that consumers and producers are less sensitive about transport costs, giving shippers a powerful incentive to increase their margins. Our estimates suggest that reducing LAC's average tariff rate to the level of the United States can reduce transport costs on average by nearly 10 percent, with countries with above the average tariffs such as Argentina and Brazil accounting for the bulk of the gains.

---

[93] See Globo On line, http://oglobo.globo.com/pais/mat/2008/03/03/anac_quer_tratado_de_ceus_abertos_na_america_do_sul-426054295.asp.

In Chapter 3, we assess what a trade agenda that incorporates transport costs can mean to the volume and diversification of the region's trade, particularly when compared to a traditional, tariffs-only agenda. At a time when, despite all the favorable winds of a China-led commodity boom, LAC's share of world trade remains clearly below its potential—both in volume and diversification—the importance of knowing the likely payoff of different trade strategies can hardly be overestimated.

Our estimates confirm that bringing down both tariffs and freight rates can have a substantial impact on both the amount and variety of goods traded by region. A 10 percent decrease in those trade costs would increase, on average, LAC's imports by 50 percent, intraregional exports by more than 60 percent, the number of imported products by 9 percent, and that of intraregional exported products by more than 10 percent.

Our findings also reveal that lower transport costs can do a lot more for LAC's trade than lower tariffs. The positive impacts of a given reduction in transport costs on intraregional exports and on the number of products exported exceed that of a similar reduction in tariffs by factors of 5 and 9, respectively. Depending on the country and the sector, this difference can be even larger. This sort of transport costs dominance over tariffs is also seen in LAC's exports to the United States.

The case studies reviewed in Chapter 4 provide real-world examples of what is at stake when an inefficient transport network imposes a heavy burden on trade. In Ecuador, we see how proximity and the time sensitiveness of a good interact to produce export opportunities and how these opportunities can be curtailed by the shortcomings in infrastructure. In Brazil, we see a story of a commodity boom where farmers have a substantial part of their rents eaten away by dysfunctional logistics. The case study of Argentina draws attention to the often forgotten fact that the export of new products to new markets requires substantial investment in transport. Mexico's case is a cautionary tale about the importance of non-policy trade costs for countries where proximity, interacting with local endowments, plays a key role in their competitive advantages.

*****

All in all, the case for expanding the scope of the region's trade agenda, with transport costs at its very center, seems very clear. What may not be clear is that we did not cover all the potential benefits of this expanded agenda. We focused on greater volumes and greater diversification of trade, but we left aside the potential political and economic benefits of better distributing the gains of trade, be that within a country or within members of a trade agreement. In an area marked by profound regional inequalities, this dimension of the trade-transport nexus cannot and should not be left outside the policy debate. True, collecting data on domestic freight is a challenging exercise—to say the least—but the policy rewards seem to be worth the effort. We see this issue as a natural follow-up to the research effort we have made in this report.[94]

To argue that transport costs should be brought into the trade agenda is, of course, much easier said than done. We see some important political and technical challenges. On the political side, the challenge is to turn the often mundane and invisible details of the transport network into something that can be perceived by politicians as generating political benefits. For instance, announcing a trade agreement has a far greater potential of attracting the voter's attention (for good or bad, these days) than building ports and railroads. Likewise, announcing a grandiose plan to take the country to the "knowledge society" tends to generate much more publicity than reducing delays at border crossings or deregulating air transportation—whatever the intrinsic economic value of those policies. On the technical side, there are, first, the well-known risks of a "push" towards transport infrastructure being interpreted as license to pursue any project. The general need for infrastructure neither exempts projects from being submitted to a rigorous cost benefit analysis, nor exempts countries from respecting their fiscal, macroeconomic and environmental constraints.[95]

A second technical challenge arises from the stringent fiscal and financial constraints that beset most governments in the region. True, the recent

[94] On this issue see, for instance, Krugman and Elizondo (1996) and Dávila, Kesel and Levy (2002).

[95] For the risks of ignoring those constraints, see Vito Tanzi (2005).

commodity boom has loosened those constraints for those that are fortunate enough to be abundant in natural resources, but, still, we are talking of governments of developing countries that have a daunting social and economic agenda ahead of them. Public and private partnerships are far from a panacea—particularly because of contractual intricacies and contingent liabilities—but experiences such as those of Chile and Brazil suggest that they can be an interesting way to reconcile the need for state coordination and intervention with its lack of funds and its management limitations.

Finally, there is the technical challenge of implementing the so-called regional transport projects that involve two or more countries, and which are plagued with externalities and coordination failures. Here there seems to be a clear role for regional initiatives such as the Initiative for Integration of Regional Infrastructure in South America (IIRSA) and the Plan Puebla Panama (PPP), which, with the support of international financial institutions such as the IDB and CAF, have been helping governments in the region to coordinate and finance infrastructure projects.[96]

The challenges are far from trivial but the payoff is clear: a region better positioned to take advantage of the growth and welfare benefits of trade.

---

[96] For a discussion of the conceptual issues behind regional infrastructure projects and the role of IIRSA, see the special issue of *Integration and Trade,* No 28, volume 12, 2008.

Data Appendix

The data used in this report come from a variety of sources. After describing the three main datasets employed, this appendix provides additional information on the data sources for each chapter.

U.S. Waterborne Databanks. U.S. Department of Transportation, Maritime Administration. Years 2000–2005. This dataset reports customs information on U.S. maritime imports (exports) from all exporting (importing) countries at the 6-digit Harmonized System level. Data include customs import value, cost of freight, insurance and other charges (excluding U.S. import duties), shipping weight, and percent of containerized shipped weight. Data are available at the port level for the origin of the shipment and at the port level for its destination.

U.S. Imports of Merchandise. U.S. Census Bureau. Years 2000–2006. This dataset reports customs information on U.S. imports from all exporting countries at the 6-digit Harmonized System level by transport mode (ocean, air). Data include customs import value, cost of freight, insurance and other charges, shipping weight, dutiable value, calculated duty and transport mode. Data are available at the country level for the origin of the shipment and at the district level for its destination.

ALADI (Latin American Association of Foreign Trade). Foreign Trade Statistics System Years 1990, 1995, 2000–2005. This dataset reports customs information for Argentina, Bolivia, Brazil, Colombia, Cuba, Chile, Ecuador, Mexico, Paraguay, Peru, Uruguay and Venezuela. Data include import values from all exporting countries at the 6-digit Harmonized System level by transport mode (ocean, air, ground and other), costs of freight, insurance and import duties. Data are available at the country level for the origin of the shipment and at the port level for its destination.

Chapter 1

ALADI, Foreign Trade Statistics System Variables constructed with the data: ad valorem freight rates, weight-to-value ratios, effective tariff rates, and trade mode composition of imports. Countries covered: Argentina, Brazil,

Chile, Paraguay, Peru and Uruguay for most of the analysis, together with Bolivia, Ecuador, Mexico and Venezuela for the trade mode composition. Years covered varies depending on the table and figure.

U.S. Imports of Merchandise. U.S. Census Bureau. Variables constructed with the data: ad valorem freight rates, weight-to-value ratios, effective tariff rates, trade mode composition of imports and revealed comparative advantage of country *j* in good *k*. Last variable is the share of product *k* in country *j*'s exports to the United States divided by the share of product *k* in total U.S. imports. Years covered varies depending on the table and figure.

Ship Analysis database. Variable used: distance between ports in nautical miles employed in Figure 1.6c. http://shipanalysis.com

Hummels and Schaur (2007). Variable used: tariff equivalent of time saving per day. This is the premium for air shipping that firms are willing to pay to avoid an additional day of ocean transport.

Trading across Borders Survey. World Bank *Doing Business 2007.* Variable used: number of days that exporters face to get goods through local transportation, customs and ports.

Chapter 2

U.S. Waterborne Databanks. The dataset is used in the third section titled "Explaining Differences in the Costs to Export" (maritime regressions) for the period 2000–2005, and in the fourth section titled "Explaining Differences in the Costs to Import" (maritime regressions), for 2005. Variables constructed with the data: maritime ad valorem freight rates, weight-to-value ratios, total volume of imports, percent of containerized shipping weight (only in the third section) and trade imbalances (only in the third section).

U.S. Imports of Merchandise. U.S. Census Bureau. The dataset is used in the third section (air regressions) for the period: 2000–2005, and in the fourth section (air regressions) for 2005. Variables constructed with the data: air ad valorem freight rates, weight-to-value ratios, total volume of imports, and effective tariff rates (the latter, for all the air and maritime regressions in all the sections).

ALADI, Foreign Trade Statistics System. The dataset is used in the fourth section. Countries and years covered are Brazil (2005), Chile (2005), Ecuador (2004), Peru (2005) and Uruguay (2005). Variables constructed with the data: maritime and air ad valorem freight rates, weight-to-value ratios, volumes of imports and effective tariff rates. Although the ALADI database includes 12 countries from Latin America, many countries do not report several of the variables used in the chapter. For example, freight rates are not reported by Mexico and Venezuela. Import duties are not reported by Bolivia, Colombia (2001–2005), Ecuador (2000–2003, 2005), Mexico, Paraguay and Venezuela. Port of entrance is not reported by Argentina, Bolivia, Chile (2000–2004) and Venezuela.

CEPII (Centre d'études prospectives et d'informations internationales) database. Variable used: great-circle distance between capitals employed in the third and fourth sections.

Ship Analysis database. Variable used: distance between ports in nautical miles employed in the third and fourth sections (maritime regressions). http://shipanalysis.com

Broda-Weinstein. Variable used: import demand elasticities employed in all the sections. The elasticities are described in detail in C. Broda and D. Weinstein (2006). Globalization and the gains from variety. *Quarterly Journal of Economics* 121(2).

Compairdata database. Variable used: number of shippers, used in the third and fourth sections (maritime regressions). This dataset reports shipping schedules for each vessel carrying cargo between each port-port pair worldwide, including the liner company operating each vessel. The data were collected for the fourth quarter of 2006.

ICAO (International Civil Aviation Organization) database. Variables used: number of airlines, used in the third and fourth sections (air regressions), and airport traffic, used in the third section (air regressions). This dataset reports the airline companies traveling between each airport-airport pair worldwide. The dataset also reports total annual freight in metric tons of each major airport in the world.

Airportcitycode.com. Variable used: airport runway length, used in the third section (air regression).

Portualia.com. Variable used: number of ports that have lifts with leverage capacity of at least 50 tons, used in the fourth section (maritime regression).

World Development Indicators, World Bank. Variables used: country area in square kilometers and the country total population (used in the fourth section, maritime regressions).

Chapter 3

ALADI, Foreign Trade Statistics System. The dataset is used for the following variables: ad valorem freight rates, effective tariff rates and bilateral imports by sector in all modes of transportation. Countries and years covered are: Argentina (2000–2005), Brazil (2000–2005), Bolivia (2001, 2004), Chile (2000–2005), Colombia (1995, 2000), Ecuador (2003, 2004), Paraguay (2000–2002), Peru (1995, 2000–2005) and Uruguay (1995, 2000–2005).

U.S. Waterborne Databanks. The dataset is used for the following variables: ad valorem freight rates, effective tariff rates and bilateral imports by sector in all modes of transportation. Years covered: 2000–2005.

CEPII (Centre d'études prospectives et d'informations internationales) database. The dataset is used for the great-circle distance between capitals, and for the dummy variables common border and common language.

Index

R

S

T